Marketing and Leasing:
OFFICE BUILDINGS

IREM Content and
Curriculum Development:

Rebecca Niday

IREM Institute of Real Estate Management

Printed in the United States of America
10 Digit: 1-57203-227-8
13 Digit: 978-1-57203-227-9

Library of Congress Cataloging-in-Publication Data

Marketing and leasing : office buildings. -- Third edition.
    pages cm
  Earlier editions published as Marketing and leasing of office space, written by Duane F. Roberts.
  Includes bibliographical references and index.
  ISBN 978-1-57203-227-9 (softcover) -- ISBN 1-57203-227-8 (softcover) 1. Office buildings--Management. 2. Offices. 3. Real estate management. 4. Office leases. 5. Landlord and tenant. I. Roberts, Duane F. Marketing and leasing of office space. II. Institute of Real Estate Management.
  HD1393.55.R63 2015
  333.33'870688--dc23
                    2014046758

ACKNOWLEDGEMENTS

We would like to thank the following Review Team for taking time from their personal and professional schedules to provide content and to review this book. Their dedication and support of IREM® are greatly appreciated!

REVIEW TEAM CHAIR

Stephen M. Cary, CPM®
[Omaha, Nebraska]

REVIEW TEAM MEMBERS

Jacqueline Harris, CPM®
[Los Angeles, California]

Sam Chanin, CPM®
[Aliso Viejo, California]

TABLE OF CONTENTS

INTRODUCTION

This book provides the information a property manager needs to successfully face the challenges of attracting and retaining office building tenants.

The following topics are covered:

- **OFFICE MARKETS.** Office building characteristics, economics of office buildings, impact of leasing on value, method of space measurement

- **MARKET ASSESSMENT.** Regional and neighborhood analysis, impact of various economic factors (e.g., occupancy, vacancy, and availability rates, supply and demand, absorption), comparison grids for establishing average market rent

- **MARKETING AND LEASING STRATEGIES.** Working with brokers, office building marketing tactics, tenant mix and placement, prospect qualification, office building lease provisions, lease negotiation and analysis

- **TENANT RETENTION.** Implementing retention strategies, resolving tenant complaints, lease expiration, and buy outs

CHAPTER 1

Understanding Office Buildings

The following is a typical timeline of an office building lease deal. The timeline below shows where we are within the process.

| Understanding Office Buildings | Assessing the Market | Developing Marketing Plans | Developing Leasing Plans | Formulating the Lease | Retaining Tenants |

A real estate manager's role in marketing and leasing has a direct impact on the value of an office building, and knowledge of office building characteristics and economic factors is critical for an effective plan. A property manager must be able to identify office building characteristics and economic factors that contribute to an effective market analysis.

What's in this chapter:

- Office Building Characteristics
- Office Building Classifications and Types
- Lease Types
- The Economics of Office Buildings
- Method of Space Measurement

OFFICE BUILDING CHARACTERISTICS

The average American worker spends about eight hours a day at work. That roughly translates into 40 hours a week and 2,080 hours a year. Considering that many Americans work for 40 years, that calculates to about 83,200 hours at work over the course of a lifetime. There is no doubt that office buildings play an integral role in the lives of individual workers and the companies for which they work.

8	40
Hours per day	Hours per week
2,080	83,200
Hours per year	Hours per life

Savvy real estate managers recognize that attracting and retaining office building tenants is key to maximizing value and meeting the owner's goals. It all begins with the target market. In order to understand the target market of an office building, it is necessary to review various characteristics of the office building property. In broad terms, the following characteristics define an office building's position in the market:

- Building classification
- Building type

Throughout the rest of this chapter, we'll explore these characteristics in more detail.

OFFICE BUILDING CLASSIFICATIONS AND TYPES

Office buildings are categorized according to their location, age, size, condition, and amenities for comparison purposes. They are generally classified as Class A, Class B, or Class C. Class type can fluctuate and change, over time, with any office building.

FIGURE 1-1: OFFICE BUILDING CLASSIFICATIONS

CLASS A	CLASS B	CLASS C

$$$	$$	$
• Command highest rents • Most attractive and prestigious • Sometimes referred to as the "100% building"	• May be similar structurally to Class A, but cannot command highest rents • Less desirable location, amenities, and so forth • Some buildings built to be Class B • Others may have been downgraded	• Substantially older • Often located on the perimeter of the central business district (CBD) • Provides basic facilities and services, thereby commanding less rent • May be close to functional obsolescence

Many factors contribute to an office building's classification and target market. Two prevailing issues are:

- Age
- Obsolescence

For example, if an older building is potentially appealing but cannot be retrofitted for advanced office systems, the building class will decline. The office building must be able to accommodate current business needs to maximize its economic potential. The importance of different attributes will vary depending on the market and changes in the economy. Additional classification factors include:

FACTOR	DESCRIPTION
Location	• Proximity to other business(es) • Accessibility (easy access, accommodates several modes of transportation, and parking) • Prestige (image, reputation, and building size)
Tenant Mix	• Tenants' reputations affect each other (mix includes type of business or trade)
Technological Infrastructure	• Examples: Increased electrical capacity and fiber optic and WiFi/WiMax hubs
Building Management	• Quality influences the value of the space and the tenants' reputations • Successful managers are responsive to tenant requests and understanding of problems
Building Services	• Type and quality of services included in the rent or available separately • Expectations driven by market and building size • Class A expectations may include: virtual or e-concierge, electronic directory board, free wireless, news board, dry cleaning services, mail room, sustainability initiatives, online work order system, coffee kiosk, food services, ATM, shoe shine, car wash and detailing, and so forth
Building Exterior and Interior	• Examples: Landscaping, lobby, elevators, corridors, mechanical systems, rest rooms, office interiors, floor configuration
HVAC Capacity	• Class A buildings will typically have digital control systems providing greater temperature control within small zones, providing for greater occupant comfort and financial efficiencies

FACTOR	DESCRIPTION
Elevator Quality and Speed	• Class A buildings will have higher-grade finishes in elevator cabs (e.g., monitors with short news and entertainment features) as well as higher speeds, thereby reducing occupant wait time
Ceiling Heights	• Class A buildings will typically have ceiling heights of nine feet or more providing a greater cube of space
Floor Load Capacity	• Class A buildings will have greater floor load capacity allowing greater density of occupancy or accommodating certain tenant types that may require more floor load capacity (e.g., law firms and/or accounting firms)

FIGURE 1-2: WORK ORDER WEBSITE BUILDING SERVICES EXAMPLE

Source: Sam Chanin, CPM®

So, what does this mean for you as a real estate manager? In order to determine your property's target market and value, you need to know how your building compares to others in the marketplace. As a real estate manager, you can influence your building's class in many ways. Higher-class buildings command higher rents and maximize value for the owner.

Q. Does every market have a Class A, Class B, and Class C?

A. Yes. Since office building classification is "relative," every market can be segmented by these classifications. However, a Class A building in a medium-sized Midwestern city may not look anything like a Class A building in a large metropolitan area, yet within its locale it would legitimately be considered Class A. Local brokers acclimate owners and tenants to the factors in a particular market that determine classification.

Q. Do Class A buildings exist outside the central business district (CBD)?

A. Yes. Outlying areas where land prices and rents might be lower attract businesses that want to reduce their occupancy costs. Business centers are constructed near highways and airports as a result of demand for office space in the suburbs.

Q. What factors might contribute to a building downgrading class?

A. Examples may include age, functional obsolescence, and shifts in the economic centers (economic obsolescence) resulting in a less than desirable location, increasingly inefficient energy usage, or failing to match competing features and amenities with new buildings in the market.

Q. What are common mistakes when upgrading building class?

A. One of the biggest mistakes is attempting to upgrade an older office building that is in a poor location. A landlord may invest a large amount of money in building modifications in an effort to attract a better tenant, but the landlord cannot overcome the building's location deficiency. Another common mistake is changing the target market instead of the building class. A Class B building due to functional obsolescence can be retrofitted to add special data ports and attract new types of technology clients, but this is just making the space appeal to a target market.

Q. How do sustainability initiatives impact building class?

A. Building class and the factors that impact building class, vary from market to market. There is no "one size fits all" approach. Remember that savvy tenants understand that sustainability initiatives, such as LEED certification, will allow them to maximize occupant comfort and realize operational cost savings. While these efforts may not change the class of a building, they will be viewed as amenities and can potentially make your building more competitive. Many states now have legislation on meeting sustainability initiatives (e.g., new buildings and public facilities must have a LEED rating) so this is an area to monitor closely for your local market.

Office buildings are also differentiated based on type of structure and use:

TYPE	DESCRIPTION

Multi-story 	• No standard definition of high-rise, mid-rise, or low-rise office buildings
	• Guidelines dependent on regional characteristics, city size, or local conception
	• High-rise may be 40 stories or more in some cities and 12 stories or more in others
	• Rental rates will vary with height and location
	  – Class A space in a high-rise building in the CBD commands highest rates per square foot (psf)
	  – Class C space in an older building on the edge of the CBD may have lowest rates psf

Garden Office Buildings 	• Usually a low-rise structure with one or two stories and no elevators • Typically located in suburban area and grouped together in office parks (located near major highways and offer abundant "free" parking) • Suburban rental rates generally lower than CBD
Flex Space 	• Single-story, may have limited mezzanine office space, often located in business parks • Designed to incorporate different configurations for both large and small space users • No common area lobbies; usually lacks high-end fixtures • Accommodates companies that need lots of less expensive space and need to combine office and warehousing (e.g., data centers, call centers)
Multi-use and Mixed-use Developments 	• Multi-use: Combines two uses (e.g., office and retail) • Mixed-use (MXD): Combines at least three different uses (refer to figure below) • MXD can sometimes result in the highest and best use of a piece of land • MXD may involve a greater degree of complexity (e.g., relationships between leaseholders, issues regarding common areas)
Medical Office Buildings (MOB) 	• Buildings whose space is leased primarily to medical and dental professionals • Space must be designed and built to meet tenants' needs for additional (sometimes specialized) plumbing and electrical wiring • Nature of clients and services they provide mandates special care in cleaning and hazardous medical waste disposal (specific responsibilities should be addressed in lease) • ADA compliance is a critical issue

TYPE	DESCRIPTION
Government Buildings 	• With privatization of government established, more opportunities available to manage public buildings or lease space to government tenants • Ability to log on to public General Services Administration (GSA) website and view a list of tenant needs and requirements – **Pros:** Huge source of revenue, variety of space needs (e.g., urban, suburban, rural, large space, small space), longer leases, no risk of insolvency – **Cons:** Tenants may have special requirements (e.g., lighting, security), space needs to be totally customizable, lower rents • Websites: *www.gsa.gov, www.fbo.gov*

FIGURE 1-3: HOW HIGH IS HIGH-RISE?

High-Rise in Large Urban Market   **High-Rise in Mid-Size Market**

Know your local market!

FIGURE 1-4: MIXED-USE DEVELOPMENT EXAMPLE

Trump Tower in New York City

Three Different Revenue-Generating Uses
1. 26 stories of office space
2. 38 stories of condominium residences
3. Upscale shopping center

Source: www.wikipedia.org

BUILDING LEASE TYPES

Another component of understanding office buildings is familiarity with the various lease types. The lease type is important because it dictates how rent is paid and how expenses are recaptured, which ultimately results in a building's value. It is also important when comparing lease proposals to ensure an "apples to apples" comparison. There are two broad types of leases:

LEASE TYPE	DESCRIPTION
Gross Lease	• Tenant pays a fixed rent • Landlord responsible for paying all property expenses (taxes, insurance, utilities, repairs) • Property expenses factored into the rent • Tenant's rent may be higher • Rents will normally adjust to higher levels to offset increased operating expenses

Net Lease	• Tenant pays a prorated share of some or all operating expenses (pass-through charges) and taxes in addition to base or minimum rent
	• Prorated share based on square feet and estimated at the beginning of the year, then divided by 12
	• Monthly charges added to monthly rent and adjusted to actual costs at the end of the year
	• Each extra "net" requires the tenant to pay for more operating costs:
	  – **Net-net (NN or double-net):** Tenant pays taxes, insurance, and possibly utilities and special assessments
	  – **Net-net-net (NNN or triple-net):** Tenant pays a prorated share of all operating expenses, taxes, insurance, utilities, and maintenance

The acronym TIM spells out how "net-ness" may be defined.

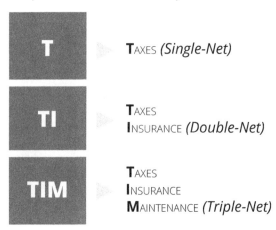

T   TAXES *(Single-Net)*

TI   TAXES
INSURANCE *(Double-Net)*

TIM   TAXES
INSURANCE
MAINTENANCE *(Triple-Net)*

Keep in mind that lease type affects the perception of rental rates. Ultimately, the market place determines rents, but if a building is marketed with a triple-net lease that allows opportunities to recapture costs, the base rent looks cheaper. On the other hand, if a gross lease is employed, with operating costs included in the rent, the stated rent will appear higher. Knowledge of specific lease types is critical to accurately understanding office buildings and how leasing affects value.

THE ECONOMICS OF OFFICE BUILDINGS

Owners invest in office buildings for a variety of reasons. To owners, these buildings may symbolize:

- Power
- Pride of ownership
- Wealth
- Financial security

But ultimately, investors own office buildings to secure a financial return measured by net operating income and periodic cash flow.

Impact of Leasing on Value

Let's take a closer look at some concepts and calculations that measure a property's financial performance and demonstrate the impact of leasing on value. Keep in mind that marketing and leasing activities affect a building's value. The real estate manager is directly involved with the building's cash flow and thus value.

Cash Flow and Pro Forma Statement of Cash Flow

Cash flow, also known as *periodic return,* is generated by the real estate investment. It is what remains after operating expenses and debt service have been deducted from the effective gross income. Remember that leases may require tenants to reimburse operating expenses of the property as a separate pass-through charge in addition to base rent. Other revenues are itemized below gross potential rental income in a separate category called expense pass-throughs, additional rent, or other scheduled income. The *pro forma statement of cash flow:*

- Is an annual cash flow statement that lists projected income and expenses in a specific format
- Includes revenue and operating expenses filtered down through net operating income (NOI) less annual debt service (ADS) to before-tax cash flow (BTCF)
- Can be adjusted to meet the unique requirements of different owners and property types
- Is often a hybrid of cash and accrual accounting, and at times will include capital items and possibly reserves for replacements

The IREM pro forma statement consists of the following items that will provide a basis for projecting through the holding period. This pro forma statement is a projection of next year's expectations.

ITEM	DESCRIPTION
Gross Potential Income (GPI)	• Income potential for the property, if it were fully leased at current market rentals
Loss to Lease	• Difference between current rents and market rents for those rents that, for any reason, exist at below-market rates • Most readily seen during the acquisition of an existing property
Vacancy and Debt Collection Loss	• Figure based on market conditions and historical experience of vacancy and collection losses for the property • Includes three items: economic vacancy (includes concessions), physical vacancy, and delinquent rents
New Rent Revenue	• Gross Potential Income minus loss to lease and vacancy and collection loss
Miscellaneous Income and Expense Reimbursements	• Can be from any source other than rents (e.g., parking)
Effective Gross Income (EGI)	• Net Rent Revenue plus miscellaneous income and expense reimbursements
Operating Expenses	• Line-by-line expenses associated with the property • Includes real estate taxes • Note: Leasing commissions should not be put in operating expenses. They are not an "expense" because they are capitalized and depreciated over the term of the lease, thereby lowering the owner's taxes.
Net Operating Income (NOI)	• Represents the amount of money that remains after operating expenses are subtracted from effective gross income • Primary measure of a property's value • Market conditions influence a property's income stream, which affects rent levels and occupancy

ITEM	DESCRIPTION
Annual Debt Service (ADS)	• Annual amount paid to service the debt on the property • Loan facts should be specified in order to calculate ADS and loan balances • Some lenders require specified percentage set-asides/reserves. Failing to maintain required reserves can result in loan default. These payments are made in addition to the principal and interest and kept by the lender until spent by the owner and funds requested from the bank based on actual costs incurred.
Capital Expenditures or Reserves for Replacement	• Not always required. It depends on the requirements of the owner. • Some owners assume that capital expenditures will be paid through cash flow or from refinancing the property. Conservative owners will set aside reserves annually for future capital costs.

FIGURE 1-5: PRO FORMA STATEMENT

```
        Gross Potential Income (GPI)
   −  Loss to Lease
   −  Vacancy and Collection Loss
   ─────────────────────────────────
   =  Net Rent Revenue
   +  Miscellaneous Income
   +  Expense Reimbursements
   ─────────────────────────────────
   =  Effective Gross Income (EGI)
   −  Operating Expenses
   ─────────────────────────────────
   =  Net Operating Income (NOI)
   −  Annual Debt Service (ADS)
   −  BLANK (Capital Expenditures or Reserves for Replacement)
   ─────────────────────────────────
   =  Before-Tax Cash Flow (BTCF)
```

The pro forma statement stops at the before-tax cash flow. *Before-tax cash flow* refers to the return an investment will realize before the income tax liability of the ownership entity. Certainly, owning real estate has income tax consequences, but that topic is best left to the owners' tax accountant or attorney.

The pro forma operating statement provides a framework for projecting future years' returns throughout the investment holding period.

In developing a management plan for an office building, the manager must consider the impact of changes on cash flow as well as NOI.

FIGURE 1-6: SAMPLE PRO FORMA STATEMENT

Pro Forma Statement
Willow Park Year 1

Income		Year 1
Gross Potential Income (GPI)		$975,000
– Loss to Lease		$21,600
– Vacancy and Collection Loss		$36,600
= Net Rent Revenue		$916,800
+ Miscellaneous Income		$45,250
+ Property Tax Reimbursement		$0
+ Utility Reimbursement		$31,000
+ CAM Reimbursement		$0
+ Other Reimbursement		$4,200
= Effective Gross Income (EGI)		$997,250
Operating Expenses		
Utilities		
Heat		$1,560
Electric		$25,000
Water and Sewer		$43,200
Total Utilities		$69,760
Maintenance		
Landscaping		$13,200
Janitorial		$37,000
Painting and Decorating		$31,200
Maintenance Labor		$31,200
Maintenance Contract		$23,800
HVAC		$7,200
Plumbing		$4,800
Electrical		$2,500
Security		$4,500
Total Maintenance		$155,400
Administration		
Management Fee		$43,600
Personnel Expense		$50,400
Office Supplies		$3,200
Telephone		$3,500
Marketing		$17,690
Total Administration		$118,390
Fixed Expenses		
Insurance		$43,400
Real Estate Taxes		$62,400
Contingent Exp		$6,000
		$0
		$0
		$0
Total Fixed Expenses		$111,800
– Total Operating Expenses		$455,350
(NOI)		**$541,900**

Q. How do you handle free rent? Is free rent the same thing as loss to lease?

A. Technically, *free rent* is a concession granted to a tenant at the beginning of the lease transaction (prevalent in a difficult economy), while *loss to lease* occurs because market rents have changed over time, or there is a desire to acquire a "brand" tenant. However, the bottom line is that from an analytical point of view we always want to arrive at an "effective rent." Since *effective rent* takes into account free rent and the rental rate (from which loss to lease is calculated), free rent and loss to lease have similar effects on the end result. It is just a matter of how you get there. Be sure to discuss these items prior to structuring the lease.

Q. What are the pros and cons of offering free rent versus half the rent for an extended period of time?

A. In either case, a concession is being granted. By offering free rent at the front-end of the lease, both landlord and tenant recognize the concession early in the process.

From the tenant's perspective, this may give the tenant opportunity to absorb costs of moving into the building before rent has to be paid. Or, it may allow the tenant to move into the building prior to the expiration of an existing lease.

From the landlord's perspective, offering free rent at the beginning of a lease term, as opposed to spreading the concession out over an extended period of time, will result in a lower valuation for that lease when recognizing the time value of money. At the same time, it will potentially create higher value for the property since future rental rates will be higher.

Rent concessions may also be spread out over the term and appear at the beginning of each year of a lease, taper off toward the end of the term, or come in toward the later years when the owner is hoping other leases will compensate for the dip in rent. One reason for spreading the free rent over the term of the lease is to mitigate the risk that the tenant will burn off the free rent and then bail out of the lease or go out of business. Another reason is to keep the tenant in the habit of paying rent each month.

Factors such as market conditions, geography, and how close an owner is to his/her holding period all play a role in structuring the lease deal. Overall, it is important to understand the owner's goals and the factors that affect value when making these decisions.

The Four Tests of Financial Performance

Throughout the development of a management plan, various financial tests are used in evaluating the performance of investment property to ensure the plan meets the owner's goals and objectives. IREM uses the following four tests of financial performance to evaluate various alternatives:

TEST	DESCRIPTION
Cash-on-Cash Rate of Return ($/$%)	• Measures investor's rate of return on the investment • Ratio that compares the cash invested in a property (equity) with the BTCF from one year • Most commonly used to show year-to-year trends in performance
Value Enhancement	• Expected value at the end of the holding period less the initial value of the investment and the cost of implementing the improvements • Partial measurement of investment return over two periods of time: acquisition and disposition
Net Present Value (NPV)	• Difference between the cost of an investment and the discounted present value of all anticipated future fiscal benefits of that investment • Can be used to compare alternative investments and rank them in order of desirability
Internal Rate of Return (IRR)	• Rate of return that equates the present value of the expected future cash flows to the initial capital invested • Discount rate that results in an NPV of zero

Valuation

Knowing the market value of an office building, as well as the factors that impact value, allows the real estate manager and the owner to make key leasing decisions. Market value can be determined in a variety of ways. Three methods are used within the real estate industry:

- Cost approach
- Comparable sales approach or market comparison approach
- Income capitalization approach

COST APPROACH

The *cost approach method* bases property value on the cost to replace the improvements on the land plus the market value of the land itself. Land value is estimated from recent sales of comparable properties or nearby vacant land. Since it is difficult for the real estate manager to accurately estimate the cost to rebuild and quantify depreciation of a property, this method has limited usefulness.

Comparable Sales Approach or Market Comparison Approach

The *comparable sales approach* uses recent sales of similar properties to determine value. Comparison factors include location, physical condition, lot size, and zoning. This method may also be limited because there is rarely a sufficient number of recent sales for the results to be reliable.

Income Capitalization Approach

The *income capitalization approach* converts a future income stream (net operating income or NOI) to an estimate of value through a process known as capitalization. It is the market valuation of a property based upon a one-year, or multiple-year, projection of income.

When using a one-year projection, the rate used to capitalize NOI is called either the overall rate of return (OAR) or the cap rate. *Cap rates* are determined from the market by examining current and past sales transactions. Cap rates are essentially estimates of return and reflect the risk inherent in the investment. **Higher cap rates result in lower values, and lower cap rates give higher values.**

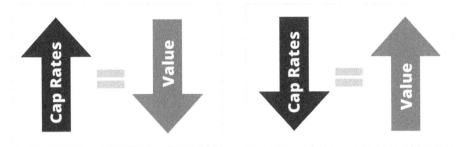

The following table shows current and historical cap rates across various property sectors.

FIGURE 1-7: SAMPLE CAP RATE INDICES

RealtyRates.com INVESTOR SURVEY - 1st Quarter 2015*
CURRENT & HISTORICAL CAP RATES INDICES
Method-Weighted[†] Property Category Indices

Year	Apts Rate	Apts BP Chg	Golf Rate	Golf BP Chg	Healthcare Senior Housing Rate	Healthcare Senior Housing BP Chg	Industrial Rate	Industrial BP Chg	Lodging Rate	Lodging BP Chg	MH/RV Park Rate	MH/RV Park BP Chg	Office Rate	Office BP Chg	Retail Rate	Retail BP Chg	Restaurant Rate	Restaurant BP Chg	Self Storage Rate	Self Storage BP Chg	Special Purpose Rate	Special Purpose BP Chg	Weighted[†] Composite Indices Rate	Weighted[†] Composite Indices BP Chg
2014	8.24	-15	11.83	-9	8.89	-1	9.03	-4	10.43	-17	9.17	-5	9.06	-22	9.26	15	11.79	-6	9.75	-20	11.24	14	9.52	-7
4th Qtr.	8.16	-3	11.74	-5	8.84	-1	8.98	-1	10.38	0	9.10	-2	9.03	2	9.20	-2	11.71	-6	9.68	-2	11.16	-4	9.46	-1
3rd Qtr.	8.19	-7	11.78	-9	8.85	-6	8.99	-5	10.38	-6	9.12	-7	9.01	-5	9.22	-5	11.76	-7	9.70	-7	11.19	-7	9.47	-6
2nd Qtr.	8.26	-8	11.87	-7	8.91	-5	9.04	-7	10.44	-7	9.19	-8	9.06	-9	9.27	-7	11.83	-5	9.77	-8	11.27	-7	9.53	-7
1st Qtr.	8.34	-4	11.94	-5	8.96	-5	9.11	2	10.51	-10	9.27	-6	9.15	-19	9.34	2	11.88	-7	9.85	-8	11.34	24	9.60	-4
2013	8.39	14	11.92	-14	8.90	5	9.07	-2	10.60	3	9.22	14	9.28	-19	9.11	-4	11.86	9	9.95	-24	11.10	1	9.58	-2
2012	8.25	-35	12.07	6	8.85	-36	9.09	-40	10.57	-24	9.08	-39	9.47	3	9.15	-13	11.77	6	10.19	-49	11.09	-4	9.60	-21
2011	8.60	-29	12.00	-22	9.21	-40	9.49	-11	10.81	7	9.48	-8	9.44	-10	9.28	-26	11.70	-14	10.69	-3	11.12	-17	9.81	-19
2010	8.89	4	12.22	5	9.62	15	9.60	-7	11.05	-7	9.55	22	9.54	16	9.54	25	11.84	12	10.72	21	11.30	0	10.00	13
2009	8.85	8	12.17	16	9.47	10	9.48	10	10.98	56	9.33	1	9.38	29	9.29	20	11.72	15	10.50	37	11.30	8	9.87	14
2008	8.77	-4	12.01	29	9.37	-16	9.38	-14	11.05	-28	9.32	-5	9.09	-16	9.09	-11	11.57	-28	10.13	20	11.22	-7	9.74	-1
2007	8.81	-45	11.72	-21	9.53	-65	9.52	-25	10.49	27	9.37	-26	9.25	-47	9.20	-12	11.85	61	9.93	-38	11.29	-24	9.75	-28
2006	9.26	12	11.93	47	10.18	15	9.77	35	10.77	-21	9.63	41	9.72	26	9.32	30	11.24	18	10.31	27	11.53	9	10.03	26
2005	9.14	14	11.46	80	10.03	-16	9.42	-30	10.50	-98	9.22	19	9.46	6	9.02	16	11.06	5	10.04	13	11.44	-30	9.77	2
2004	9.00	-19	10.66	28	10.19	-37	9.72	19	10.71	56	9.03	-48	9.40	-4	8.86	-19	11.01	-15	9.91	-4	11.74	-30	9.75	-19
2003	9.19	-2	10.38	-32	10.56	64	9.53	33	11.69	26	9.51	-11	9.44	1	9.05	-18	11.16	8	10.04	-53	12.04	105	9.94	12
2002	9.21	-40	10.70	18	9.92	-39	9.20	-61	11.13	98	9.62	-60	9.43	-35	9.23	-62	11.08	-3	10.57	-12	10.99	-177	9.82	-41
2001	9.61	64	10.52	133	10.31	90	9.81	16	10.87		10.22	-68	9.78	-35	9.85	-53	11.11	47	10.69	13	12.76	32	10.23	21
2000	8.97		9.19		9.41		9.65		9.89		10.90		10.13		10.38		10.64		10.56		12.44		10.01	

[†] Weighted by methodology: Band-of-Investment, DCR Technique, Sales Survey
* Further weighted by property category

Q. How do you find capitalization rates?

A. This is a very common question. Determining the cap rate requires a high level of skill and experience because a small error can significantly impact the resulting value. The real estate manager should develop relationships with appraisers, lenders, and brokers. Cap rates are driven by the market and can be established in three primary ways:

- Appraisers are a good source of cap rates because of their experience and training. They can calculate cap rates, adjust NOI, and estimate the market value of a property with greater skill than someone with limited training. Appraisers are frequently looking for reliable operating expense and vacancy data that real estate managers have. Developing relationships with one another will benefit both parties.

- Another valuable source for capitalization rate information is found in the broker and lender sectors in the industry. Similar to the appraisal community, brokers and lenders are also seeking reliable operating expense and vacancy data.

- If you seek to determine a cap rate for a specific property yourself, it is a good idea to find and compare recent sales of similar properties in the same market. By obtaining the purchase price and NOI from these sales, you can calculate a range of cap rates for the area.

If comparable sales are not available, cap rates can be determined using a method known as *mortgage equity analysis*. This method is explored in detail in the IREM "Investment Real Estate Financing and Valuation—Part One (ASM603)" and "Investment Real Estate Financing and Valuation—Part Two (ASM604)" courses.

Resources:

Visit *www.realtyrates.com* for additional information on capitalization rates and current trends.

When the income capitalization approach is used, the property income (I), as NOI, is divided by the capitalization rate (R) to determine property value (V). The IRV formula is shown here:

Net Operating Income (I) ÷ Capitalization Rate (R) = Estimated Market Value (V)

Selecting an appropriate cap rate is essential. The higher the cap rate, the lower the value and vice versa.

If a property's annual NOI is $700,000 and the current cap rate is 10 percent, the value would be $7,000,000.

$700,000 ÷ 0.10 = $7,000,000

If the cap rate is only one-half percent lower (9.5 percent), the value will be very different.

$700,000 ÷ 0.095 = $7,368,421

DISCOUNTED CASH FLOW METHOD

While the income capitalization approach converts a single year's NOI to an estimate of value, the *discounted cash flow* method determines the present value of a property by discounting all the future fiscal benefits of the real estate over a predetermined holding period. Instead of using a capitalization rate, a discount rate is used. Discount rates are always greater than cap rates because they must reflect not only the risk of the investment, but the risk of inflation associated with holding a property over a period of time.

The discounted cash flow method is discussed in detail in the IREM "Investment Real Estate Financing and Valuation—Part One (ASM603)" and "Investment Real Estate Financing and Valuation—Part Two (ASM604)" courses.

Management Responsibilities

The real estate manager's primary responsibility is to the owner. Ultimately, the goal is to increase net operating income by maximizing occupancy at the highest rents possible while controlling operating costs. Rental rates determine office building income which, in turn, affects the property's value.

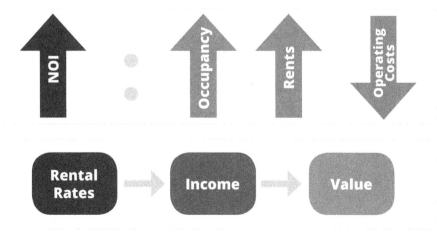

The real estate manager has an obligation to the tenants as well as to the owner. It is important to address the following challenges tenants face in order to maintain a profitable office building:

- Accommodate space needs of tenants who grow
- Retain tenants who downsize their work forces or encourage their staff members to work at home
- Protect the physical building and the people who work there while maintaining reasonable access for tenants' customers and public
- Be aware of how tenant bankruptcy can affect leasing:
    - Know your state laws on forcible entry and detainer
    - Understand a landlord's limitation with regard to collecting past-due rent while a tenant is in bankruptcy
    - Identify that the availability of the space will be affected as long as a tenant is in bankruptcy
- Stay informed of financial changes in the company:
    - Review employee rosters and look for hiring, firing, and layoff trends
    - Track frequent or habitual late payments; review lease and tenant financial statements as needed
    - Track performance of public companies online
    - Fulfill landlord's lessee obligation

tips

If you successfully meet the tenants' needs, you will successfully meet the owner's needs.

Maintaining and improving the building makes it attractive to tenants who will pay higher rents, which increases the value of the property. A real estate manger must understand the owner's objectives for the investment and manage the property accordingly.

METHOD OF SPACE MEASUREMENT

A real estate manager must be clear on the space measurement method in order to compare the property to others in the market and communicate effectively with owners and tenants. Methods of space measurement can affect:

- Rent
- Gross Potential Income (GPI)
- Value

Computer-Assisted Design and Drafting (CAD) Diagram

The market standard for space measurement is the use of computer-assisted design and drafting (CAD) systems. The CAD shows detailed space specifications that allow both the tenant and management to work from the same assumptions.

FIGURE 1-8: CAD DIAGRAM

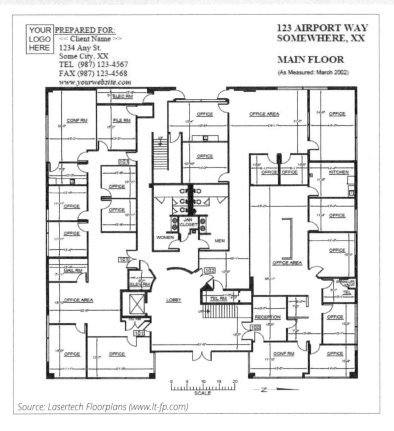

Source: Lasertech Floorplans (www.lt-fp.com)

Now more than ever, office building managers make CAD diagrams available on the property's website. Often, potential tenants won't put your building on their short list if you can't provide a CAD. Also, potential tenants' vendors ask for a copy of the CAD file to assess telecommunication needs, where to put outlets, and so forth. CAD files are an increasingly valuable tool in the marketing and leasing process. Multiple Smartphone and Tablet apps are available for CAD review as well.

tips

BOMA Standard

The Building Owners and Managers Association International (BOMA) has developed a standard for measuring office building space that is widely accepted in the industry. Over time, this standard has been revised to reflect market need and the evolution of office building design; it is referred to as *Office Buildings: Standard Methods of Measurement and Calculating Rentable Area (2010)*. The BOMA measurement standard offers two options. Both methods produce the same total rentable area of any building and utilize similar space classifications and boundaries.

METHOD	DESCRIPTION
Method A (legacy method)	• Calculates the rentable areas of the building and each of its floor levels • Continues many features of the predecessor standard, ANSI/BOMA Z65.1-1996
Method B (single load factor method)	• A new calculation applied to the occupant area of each floor determines the rentable area and is the same for all floors of buildings • Requires diligent on-going documentation (using tools such as CAD)

Source: Office Buildings: Standard Methods of Measurement and Calculating Rentable Area (2010), *www.boma.org*

Resources:

Visit the Building Owners and Managers Association International (BOMA) at *www.boma.org* for additional information and detailed calculations.

Note that there are four vendors who provide interpretation work for BOMA International's Floor Measurement standard:

1. American Building Calculations *(www.abcalc.biz)*
2. Extreme Measures *(www.xmeasures.com)*
3. Stevenson Systems *(www.stevensonsystems.com)*
4. Lasertech Floorplans *(www.lasertechfloorplans.com)*

Terms

- **Rentable area of a building:** The entire interior floor area less vertical penetrations through the floor (elevators, stairways, ventilation shafts)
- **Usable area of a building:** The rentable area less certain common areas shared by all tenants (washrooms, hallways, storage areas)

- **Floor Usable Area:** The sum of usable areas, store areas, and building common areas on a floor
- **Floor Common Area:** The areas on a floor such as washrooms, maintenance closets, mechanical rooms, and elevator lobbies that are used by more than one tenant on that floor
- **Usable area of a tenant's leased office space:** The area bounded by the partitions that separate one tenant's space from another (this may comprise portions of a floor, an entire floor, or multiple floors of a building)
- **Rentable area of a tenant's leased office space:** The space on which the tenant pays rent (usually includes certain common areas)

Source: Standard Method for Measuring Floor Area in Office Buildings (ANSI/BOMA Z65.1 – 1996).

FIGURE 1-9: USABLE, RENTABLE, AND GROSS AREA

Major Vertical Floor Penetrations	Common Areas	Office Space
Elevator		
	Public Corridor	
Elevator		
Elevator		
Air Ducts and Pipe Shafts	Public Washroom	

USABLE AREA

RENTABLE AREA

GROSS AREA

R/U Ratio

To calculate the tenant's rentable area (the area on which rent is paid), multiply the tenant's usable area by a Rentable/Useable (R/U) ratio. The R/U ratio is the rentable area of a floor divided by the usable area of that same floor.

Floor Rentable Area ÷ Floor Usable Area = Floor R/U Ratio

Basic Rentable Area = Usable Area × Floor R/U Ratio

**Building R/U Ratio = Building Rentable Area ÷
(Building Rentable Area – Basic Rentable Area of Building Common Area)**

R/U Ratio = Floor R/U Ratio × Building R/U Ratio

Rentable Area = Basic Rentable Area × Building R/U Ratio

A pro rata share of the building's common areas is added to the basic rentable area to arrive at the tenant's total rentable square feet. A larger R/U ratio indicates a higher rent for the usable areas.

On floors with multiple tenants, an *add-on* or *load factor* is used to charge the tenant for a percentage of the common areas, so the total square footage leased is equal to the floor's rentable area. Using the rentable area instead of the usable area allows the manager to charge a lower square foot rental rate on a greater number of square feet instead of a higher rate for a smaller area. Also, the owner can now rent a greater proportion of the gross area.

Generally, the R/U factor is used to allot equitable portions of the operating expenses among the existing tenants. However, once the R/U factor is developed, it may not, in all cases, be used to determine rents. Some buildings have high R/U factors that exceed the average in the market. If the calculated R/U factor is higher than the market, the owner may need to lower the rent per square foot, as the market will determine the limits of rent.

tips

Tenant improvement allowances are based on usable space, not rentable space.

tips

Consider adding re-measurement rights for significant building modifications. This gives the owner greater flexibility to recover costs associated with major modifications to common areas.

Space Measurement Impact

Accurate space measurement is extremely important, as rent charges are based on rentable square feet. Even minor measurement errors can have a tremendous impact on the owner's bottom line over time. Consider the following example.

Example:

An error was made in measuring a 22-story office building. The floors were measured to the window mullion rather than the window glass, causing a one inch error on each side of the building in favor of the tenants. The correct measurement of each floor is 92 feet by 182 feet for a total of 16,744 rentable square feet per floor.

The measurement error in feet is (Note: recall that there are 12 inches per foot):

2/12 = .17 foot

The measurement error per floor is:

Actual sq ft for each floor	(92 × 182) = 16,744 SF
- Measured sq ft for each floor	(92 - .17 = 91.83) × (182 - .17 = 181.83) = 16,697 SF
= Measurement error per floor	47 SF per floor error
x Number of floors	22
= Sq ft error for building	1,034 SF error for building

Assuming an average rental rate of $15.00 per rentable square foot, the loss of revenue over a five-year holding period is:

Sq ft error for building	1,034 SF error for building
x Sq ft rental rate	15.00 per SF rental rate
= Annual loss of revenue	$15,510 annual loss of revenue
x Number of years	5
= Total loss of revenue	$77,550 total loss of revenue

IPMS—Office Building

The BOMA Standard is one of many different standards currently in use in most real estate markets in the US. There are numerous other standards in use globally. Such standards are known and recognized by those active within each market, but tend to be obscure or even contradictory to investors, managers and occupiers from outside those markets. This lack of transparency may discourage some players from approaching other markets, inhibiting investment in particular markets.

The International Property Measurement Standards Coalition (IPMSC) was established during a World Bank meeting in 2013, to specifically address this disparity in measurement standards. The IPMSC is comprised of over 50 international advocacy and educational organizations, including IREM. Its mandate was to develop an international standard for measuring office space that will be globally accepted in the industry. While available to be adopted as a new standard, the IPMS is intended to offer a means to translate the area of an office property calculated using different local standards into an internationally recognized metric.

Assembling a team of subject matter experts from around the world to form a Standards Setting Committee (SSC), the IPMSC was motivated to create a unique global standard, rather than copying or selecting an existing standard. Meeting regularly, via telephone and in-person conferences, the SSC examined different standards, debated logical and reasonable approaches to establishing applicable metrics, and evaluated various solutions, in order to create the IPMS-Office Building standard. This standard provides a bridge from whichever local standard is being used to a standard any investor or occupier would be familiar with.

IPMS—Office Building adopts three basic area definitions, generally described as follows:

IPMS 1—comprising the overall area of the building, comparable to the gross area under the BOMA standard.

IPMS 2—representing the area of the interior of the building, segregated into eight distinct components.

IPMS 3—representing the area assigned for the exclusive use of an occupier.

The complete definition and description of each area can be found in the formal IPMS —Office Building document, which may be downloaded at ***http://ipmsc.org***.

It is important to keep in mind some of the key elements of the IPMS. The three area definitions are not intended to be cumulative, that is IPMS 2 + IPMS 3 does not equal IPMS 1. IPMS is only intended to confirm the size of a building, not its value or revenue-generating potential; such matters are affected by many different variables and market considerations. IPMS 2 and IPMS 3 employ the "internal dominant face" as the standard approach to measuring exterior perimeter dimensions.

CHAPTER 1:
Resources

Websites

www.realtyrates.com

www.boma.org (Building Owners and Managers Association International [BOMA])

www.abcalc.biz (American Building Calculations)

www.xmeasures.com (Extreme Measures)

www.stevensonsystems.com (Stevenson Systems)

www.lasertechfloorplans.com (Lasertech Floorplans)

CHAPTER 2

Assessing the Market

This book follows the typical timelines of an office building lease deal. The timeline below shows where we are within the process.

| Understanding Office Buildings | **Assessing the Market** | Developing Marketing Plans | Developing Leasing Plans | Formulating the Lease | Retaining Tenants |

An accurate market analysis allows the real estate manager to set appropriate rental rates and identify the target market in order to meet the owner's goals and objectives. A property manager must be able to conduct a market analysis to position the office building within the context of the local market.

What's in this chapter:

- Market Analysis
- Regional Analysis (macro market)
- Neighborhood Analysis (micro market)
- Economics
- Property Analysis
- Comparison Grid Analysis

MARKET ANALYSIS

CHECKLIST: MARKETING 101

☐ **DEFINE THE TARGET MARKET:** One of the first steps in the marketing process is to identify that portion of the total office market you wish to attract as tenants. By defining the profile of your desired tenants and identifying where those tenants can be found, you can more narrowly focus your marketing efforts.

　　☐ Conduct a comparison grid analysis (discussed later in this chapter) that provides information about your building in comparison to other buildings that also appeal to your target market

　　☐ Survey the tenants already in your building, paying particular attention to the opinions of the tenants you especially want to keep (e.g., Who do they do business with, and who would they like to have as neighbors? Why did they select this space?). Rate features such as location, transportation, parking, elevators, building services, proximity to other businesses, and so forth.

Continued on next page

CHECKLIST: MARKETING 101 *(Continued)*

☐ **POSITION BUILDING:** Once you've defined your target market, it is important to identify the characteristics of your building that will appeal to that segment of the market and to design your marketing campaign to reach that segment. By determining what group or groups to appeal to, and how best to communicate with them, you maximize the return on your marketing dollar.

☐ **DIFFERENTIATE PRODUCT:** Next, identify those qualities of your building that are different from your competitors' buildings and how you can use these differences in your marketing message.

In order to make informed decisions regarding marketing and leasing activities, you must define and evaluate the market in its current state and estimate how it may change in the future.

Market analysis is an evaluation of the competition and the property's position in the marketplace. It is the first step in marketing and leasing activities, and it is a critical component of preparing a management plan. But why is it so important? Ultimately, the information that is analyzed determines the rental rates that will maximize occupancy levels and income for the office building.

CHECKLIST: MARKET ANALYSIS

A market analysis helps answer the following questions:

☐ Who is the target audience for my building?

☐ What tenants are/are not represented in the market at this time?

☐ What rental rates are currently charged in the market?

☐ What are the trends in the market going forward?

☐ How does the neighborhood impact the property?

☐ What are the regional political, social, and economic trends?

☐ How will regional and neighborhood trends influence the property?

☐ How can good management take advantage of these trends?

☐ What is the demand for this type of property?

☐ How does this demand relate to the ready supply?

☐ How will supply change within the hold period?

☐ What is the absorption for the property type within the neighborhood?

☐ What describes the market for the property demographically?

The office market can be divided into two factors:

1. Potential office tenants
2. Buildings that compete with the subject property

The market analysis explores these factors in the context of the following components:

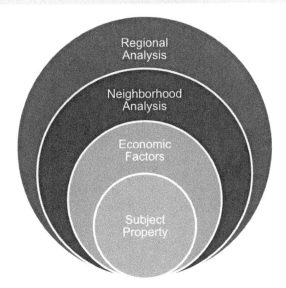

FIGURE 2-1: MARKET ANALYSIS COMPONENTS

Regional Analysis

Neighborhood Analysis

Economic Factors

Subject Property

As part of the market analysis, the real estate manager must:

- Study the region and neighborhood in which the subject property is located
- Analyze the economic factors and demographic profile
- Evaluate the property itself
- Relate the property to the competitive market and its neighborhood

REGIONAL ANALYSIS

A *region* (also called the "macro market") is the market area in which changes in economic conditions are likely to affect the fiscal performance of a particular office building. Often, the region is defined as the metropolitan statistical area (MSA) in which a property is located.

Following is a sample MSA map of Pennsylvania. Each metropolitan area shown could easily be a "region."

FIGURE 2-2: MSA MAP OF PENNSYLVANIA

Source: U.S. Census Bureau MSA Map of the United States (www.census.gov).

A *regional analysis* (also known as the "macro market analysis") will determine the economic strength of the area in general, including:

- Employment information
- Per capita income
- Types of businesses

It should include an evaluation of the economic conditions and demographics of the region.

---

tips

When conducting a regional analysis, look for trends that might appear by analyzing several years of data.

Economics

Economic conditions influence rental rates as well as the choice of marketing techniques. For example, the following market area information can be used to pinpoint trends:

- Employment base
- Population
- Rent levels
- Vacancy rates

Governmental controls that affect real estate, such as property tax rates, must also be considered. Also, more and more local governments are placing restrictions on development in order to control urban and suburban sprawl.

The U.S. Census Bureau provides "America's Economy," a Smartphone and Tablet app that provides updated statistics on the U.S. economy.

tips

Demographics

Demography is the study of the various socioeconomic factors related to populations. Since a region's economy is controlled by its residents and businesses, it is important to study its demographics. For office buildings, significant demographic factors include:

- Median age
- Population growth
- Education levels
- Employment by industry type

Population data is important to businesses since they relate to labor needs. Changes in population size and density due to births, deaths, and movement of people into and out of the region are important to measure because population growth and employment rates affect the demand for office space. Savvy commercial real estate managers track the relationship between population growth (or decline) and the area's office-oriented business activity.

Knowing the trends in the labor market of your property is a tool that helps you understand the long-term outlook of the market, as jobs are a key driver of office building occupancy.

It is also important to stay up-to-date on industries that are growing, and familiarity with the *North American Industry Classification System (NAICS)* is key. NAICS is the standard used by federal statistical agencies in classifying business establishments for the purpose of collecting, analyzing, and publishing statistical data related to the U.S. business economy. Geographic information system (GIS) reports use NAICS codes, and Internet listing sites, such as CoStar, use them as well. Additionally, NAICS codes are important in identifying a tenant's "use" as it is written in the lease. Significant NAICS codes that are important to the office market include the "FIRE" (finance, insurance, real estate) as well as Services and Government categories.

FIGURE 2-3: NAICS CODES

53	**Real Estate and Rental Leasing**[T]
531	**Real Estate**[T]
5311	**Lessors of Real Estate**
53111	Lessors of Residential Buildings and Dwellings
531110	Lessors of Residential Buildings and Dwellings
53112	Lessors of Nonresidential Buildings (except Miniwarehouses)
531120	Lessors of Nonresidential Buildings (except Miniwarehouses)
53113	Lessors of Miniwarehouses and Self-Storage Units
531130	Lessors of Miniwarehouses and Self-Storage Units
53119	Lessors of Other Real Estate Property
531190	Lessors of Other Real Estate Property
5312	**Offices of Real Estate Agents and Brokers**[T]
53121	Offices of Real Estate Agents and Brokers[T]
531210	Offices of Real Estate Agents and Brokers
5313	**Activities Related to Real Estate**[T]
53131	Real Estate Property Managers
531311	Residential Property Managers
531312	Nonresidential Property Mangers
53132	Offices of Real Estate Appraisers
531320	Offices of Real Estate Appraisers
53139	Other Activities Related to Real Estate
531390	Other Activities Related to Real Estate
532	**Rental and Leasing Services**[T]
5321	**Automotive Equipment Rental and Leasing**[T]

Source: U.S. Census Bureau *(www.census.gov)*.

The American Fact Finder website *(http://factfinder.census.gov/)* is the U.S. government's most comprehensive census research tool for the general public. It can be used for the following information:

INFORMATION	DESCRIPTION
Community Facts	Basic demographic, social, and economic data on your city, town, country, state, or ZIP code area
People	Age, sex, income, poverty, education
Housing	Housing units, household type, value of home
Business and Government	Annual payroll, sales and receipts, number of employees
Specific Data	Access data from a variety of Census Bureau Data sources

FIGURE 2-4: SAMPLE DEMOGRAPHIC DATA

Subject	Chicago city, Illinois	
	Number	Percent
EMPLOYMENT STATUS		
Population 16 years and over	2,215,574	100.0
In labor force	1,358,054	61.3
Civilian labor force	1,357,461	61.3
Employed	1,220,040	55.1
Unemployed	137,421	6.2
Percent of civilian labor force	10.1	(X)
Armed Forces	593	0.0
Not in labor force	857,520	38.7
Females 16 years and over	1,158,277	100.0
In labor force	650,844	56.2
Civilian labor force	650,736	56.2
Employed	586,047	50.6
Own children under 6 years	234,351	100.0
All parents in family in labor force	124,850	53.3
COMMUTING TO WORK		
Workers 16 years and over	1,192,139	100.0
Car, truck, or van -- drove alone	597,598	50.1
Car, truck, or van -- carpooled	172,722	14.5
Public transportation (including taxicab)	310,924	26.1
Walked	67,556	5.7
Other means	15,174	1.3
Worked at home	28,165	2.4
Mean travel time to work (minutes)	35.2	(X)
Employed civilian population 16 years and over	1,220,040	100.0
OCCUPATION		
Management, professional, and related occupations	408,486	33.5
Service occupations	202,335	16.6
Sales and office occupations	329,718	27.0
Farming, fishing, and forestry occupations	1,108	0.1
Construction, extraction, and maintenance occupations	80,245	6.6
Production, transportation, and material moving occupations	198,148	16.2

Source: U.S. Census Bureau (www.census.gov).

Another source of market conditions is the Federal Reserve "Blue Book" which presents the Federal Reserve Board staff's analysis of monetary policy alternatives.

Resources:

Trend data is available for purchase from third-party providers such as *www.demographicsnow.com* or *www.siteselection.com*.

FIGURE 2-5: SAMPLE DEMOGRAPHIC DATA (CONT.)

Subject	Chicago city, Illinois	
	Number	Percent
INDUSTRY		
Agriculture, forestry, fishing and hunting, and mining	1,079	0.1
Construction	53,460	4.4
Manufacturing	159,554	13.1
Wholesale trade	38,215	3.1
Retail trade	108,245	8.9
Transportation and warehousing, and utilities	82,650	6.8
Information	41,362	3.4
Finance, insurance, real estate, and rental and leasing	111,130	9.1
Professional, scientific, management, administrative, and waste management services	166,094	13.6
Educational, health and social services	232,324	19.0
Arts, entertainment, recreation, accommodation and food services	103,263	8.5
Other services (except public administration)	63,557	5.2
Public administration	59,107	4.8
CLASS OF WORKER		
Private wage and salary workers	990,694	81.2
Government workers	173,920	14.3
Self-employed workers in own not incorporated business	52,749	4.3
Unpaid family workers	2,677	0.2
INCOME IN 1999		
Households	1,061,964	100.0
Less than $10,000	146,192	13.8
$10,000 to $14,999	71,103	6.7
$15,000 to $24,999	132,339	12.5
$25,000 to $34,999	133,670	12.6
$35,000 to $49,999	171,140	16.1
$50,000 to $74,999	188,700	17.8
$75,000 to $99,999	95,162	9.0
$100,000 to $149,999	75,743	7.1
$150,000 to $199,999	21,884	2.1
$200,000 or more	26,031	2.5
Median household income (dollars)	38,625	(X)
With earnings	850,095	80.0
Mean earnings (dollars)	56,313	(X)
With Social Security income	229,915	21.6
Mean Social Security income (dollars)	10,469	(X)
With Supplemental Security Income	72,143	6.8
Mean Supplemental Security Income (dollars)	6,533	(X)
With public assistance income	73,415	6.9
Mean public assistance income (dollars)	2,543	(X)
With retirement income	129,550	12.2
Mean retirement income (dollars)	17,011	(X)

NEIGHBORHOOD ANALYSIS

A *neighborhood,* or *micro market, analysis* is more narrowly focused than a regional analysis. It should evaluate the economic conditions of the smaller area, including local employment, rent levels, and office vacancy rates.

An office building's "neighborhood" is the micro market area in which the building competes for tenants. You are competing for tenants on the basis of such factors as:

- Location
- Rent

- Age
- Accessibility
- Quality and type of construction
- Amenities
- Transportation
- Appearance

The neighborhood for a particular office building in a suburb may be a large geographic area; for a building located in a Central Business District (CBD), it may consist of only a few blocks.

A neighborhood analysis should include the following:

- Selling points and undesirable features of the surrounding area
    - Effects on an office building's productivity
    - Knowledge of what appeals to different businesses helps managers identify prospective tenants
- Location of the competition
    - One of the most crucial aspects of market analysis
    - Proximity of the competition to your building is important (show competing properties on a map)
- Cycles of aging and rejuvenation
    - Influence a neighborhood's competitive position
    - Important in identifying trends
        ◊ Growth evidenced by new construction
        ◊ Decline evidenced by vacancies and poorly maintained buildings

Government Regulations

Sound judgments about a neighborhood, and an office building within its boundaries, cannot be made without knowledge of government restrictions. Guidelines include the following:

- Review zoning, pending changes for land use, and building code revisions regularly, since incompatible land use can destroy the local value of a neighborhood
- Consider tax burdens
- Examine the local structure of assessed values and tax rates for their effect on the value of office buildings
- Study all city planning and urban renewal projects that concern a building's neighborhood
- Remember programs of land reutilization can have a major impact (direct or indirect) on a neighborhood as well as overall market trends (e.g., major redevelopment can affect utility service and force property owners to make major investments to accommodate the change)
- Review "FAR" Floor Area Ratios

Master planning helps identify future supply potential.

Fieldwork

Interviews, surveys, and focus groups can also be conducted to gain insight into the kinds of businesses that are moving or expanding, which has a direct impact on prospective tenants for a particular office building. This is particularly important when doing a neighborhood analysis. Additional sources of information include financial institutions and utility companies.

Research Methods

One can use a myriad of resources to analyze the region, neighborhood, and demographic profile for a specific office building. A wealth of information is available online from the following sources:

- Local and federal government
- Independent vendors of market research data
- Local not-for-profit neighborhood development agencies
- National not-for-profit institutes

CHECKLIST: REGIONAL MARKET RESEARCH COMPONENTS

Regional Data: Geographic Boundaries

- ☐ Macro economy
    - ☐ Population: numbers, direction, trends
    - ☐ Employment: FIRE (finance, insurance, real estate), administrative
    - ☐ Retail sales revenues
    - ☐ Real estate demographics: supply, demand, absorption, rents, development, and building permits
    - ☐ Transportation
    - ☐ Capital markets

CHECKLIST: NEIGHBORHOOD MARKET RESEARCH COMPONENT

Neighborhood Data: Geographic Boundaries

- ☐ Limits (use a map with the neighborhood defined by boundaries)
- ☐ Micro economy
- ☐ Land uses
    - ☐ 100% location of competitive product
    - ☐ 100% buildings and competition
    - ☐ Subject location
    - ☐ Supply, demand, absorption, and rents
    - ☐ Zoning, entitlements

Resources:

CCIM Institute, an investment-oriented affiliate of the National Association of Realtors, offers many research services on their "Site to Do Business" website: *www.stdbonline.com*. To get full access, you must be a CCIM Institute Member.

FIGURE 2-6: SOURCES OF INFORMATION

Source	Description
American Fact Finder *www.factfinder2.census.gov*	• Population size, density, distribution • Population forecasts • Age, education, and family size • Per capita income, disposable income • Consumer spending and savings
U.S. Bureau of Economic Analysis *www.bea.gov*	• Reports on regional business activity and personal income • Employment data on available labor force, types of jobs, area employers • Forecasts of expanding job markets
State Agencies and Local Governments *www.statelocalgov.net*	• State retail taxing authority • Zoning laws and use restrictions • Availability or scarcity of space zoned office and retail
Local Chambers of Commerce	• Local tax regulations • Variety of companies and industries • Strength and vitality of businesses

ECONOMICS

In addition to the regional and neighborhood analyses, it is important to examine the economic characteristics of the area and their effect on the real estate market. Demand for office space must be projected and related to supply. Vacancy rates and absorption provide insight into the economic environment of the area.

Occupancy, Vacancy, and Availability Rates

The *occupancy rate* is the amount of space that is occupied, expressed as a percentage of the total supply of office space.

Amount of Occupied Space ÷ Total Amount of Available Space × 100
= Occupancy Rate

Example:

If a building has 500,000 square feet, and 400,000 square feet is leased, the occupancy rate is 80%:

$400,000 ÷ 500,000 × 100 = 80\%$

When the occupancy rate is subtracted from 100 percent, the difference is the *vacancy rate*. It is the amount of vacant space expressed as a percentage of the total supply of office space.

Amount of Vacant Space ÷ Total Amount of Available Space × 100
= Vacancy Rate

Example:

Using the example above, the vacancy rate would be 20%:

$100,000 ÷ 500,000 × 100 = 20\%$

The *availability rate* includes vacancies as well as space that is occupied but available (e.g., sublease space, buildings under construction).

tips

Note that brokerage houses report availability rates differently, so it is important to understand the assumptions used when comparing various rates.

Supply and Demand

Supply refers to the quantity of occupied and unoccupied space available in a particular real estate market at a given time.

Demand is measured by the amount of occupied space plus the amount of vacancy that is expected when market rents are stable.

For each possible supply and demand relationship, a specific fundamental rule applies to rent level expectations:

- **SUPPLY > DEMAND:** Rent levels are likely to decrease when demand (including vacancy) is less than supply
- **SUPPLY = DEMAND:** Rent levels are stable when demand equals supply (including vacancy)
- **SUPPLY < DEMAND:** Rent levels are likely to increase when demand (including vacancy) is greater than supply

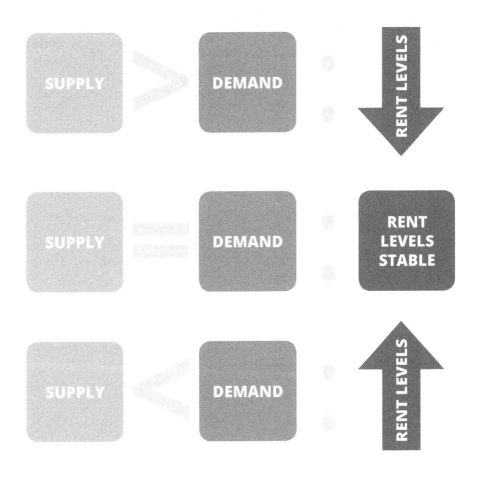

The point at which demand equals supply is known as the *equilibrium point*. Since supply and demand constantly shift, equilibrium rarely lasts for long periods of time.

The rents referred to in these rules are *effective* rents. For example, if demand in a market is less than supply, quoted rents may not change, but rental concessions may increase. The net effect is that effective rents decrease.

It is important to note that the rules of supply and demand as shown above do not take inflation into account. In real life, supply/demand imbalances cause rents to rise slower or faster than the inflation rate. If the market is in equilibrium, rent levels would increase at the rate of inflation.

If supply exceeds demand, rents are expected to rise slower than the inflation rate. If demand exceeds supply, rents are expected to rise faster than the inflation rate.

Q&A: Supply and Demand

Q. Why is supply and demand important?
A. It all comes down to setting appropriate rental rates. When supply is less than demand, it is a landlord's market. There is less competition for tenants, therefore the value and rent of the space increase.

On the other hand, when supply is greater than demand, it is a tenant's market. Increased competition for tenants leads to a decline in rents and slow leasing activity.

CHECKLIST: SOURCES OF DEMAND

☐ **INTERNAL EXPANSION:** Tenants in the local market who are experiencing internal growth and require additional space

☐ **UPWARD MOBILITY:** Tenants experiencing success in their businesses seek out upgraded office space

☐ **NEW BUSINESS FORMATIONS:** Formation of new businesses makes up an integral part of the demand equation

☐ **RELOCATING BUSINESSES (IN-MIGRATION):** Businesses that want to establish offices in the market area studied

Net Absorption

Absorption is the net change in the amount of occupied space from one period to the next, normally a year. It accounts for both construction of new space and demolition or removal from the market of existing space. It is measured in rentable square feet, and vacancy is equal to the available square feet. Absorption data is typically calculated over an entire MSA and its individual submarkets.

	Square feet vacant at the beginning of the period
+	**Square feet constructed new during the period**
–	**Space demolished, or removed from the market by a change of use, during the period**
–	**Space vacant at the end of the period**
=	**Space absorbed during the period (absorption)**

Absorption can be either positive or negative.

Example:

	Square feet vacant at the beginning of the period		2,000,000
+	Square feet constructed new during the period	+	150,000
–	Space demolished during the period	–	30,000
–	Space vacant at the end of the period	–	2,050,000
=	Space absorbed during the period (absorption)	=	70,000

Absorption rate is determined by dividing the absorption of space by the total supply of available space in the market.

**Space Absorbed ÷ Total Supply of Available Space at the End of the Period
= Absorption Rate**

Consider the following:

- When supply is less than demand, occupancy increases and absorption is positive
- When supply is greater than demand, occupancy decreases and absorption is negative

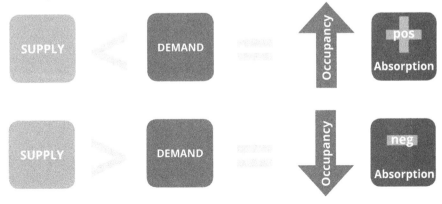

A negative absorption can reflect changes in the marketplace, such as a sudden lack of jobs due to a large company closing.

Historical data, coupled with current supply and demand data, can help estimate the time needed for the space in a given office building to be absorbed.

EXAMPLE	ABSORPTION USE
Proposed Project	• Predict leasing activity to back up a development plan and obtain financing
Existing Building	• Establish a rental schedule • Estimate the amount of space to be rented over a given period of time for the purpose of budgeting

FIGURE 2-7: ABSORPTION DATA (SQ FT)

Submarket (size)	Year -4	Year -3	Year -2	Year -1
Submarket #1 (5,891,298)	294,565	(176,739)	(235,652)	(206,195)
Submarket #2 (3,135,201)	30,300	37,046	43,890	50,163
Submarket #3 (14,027,833)	1,400,788	1,350,850	1,401,500	1,402,346
Submarket #4 (9,810,979)	(686,769)	(588,659)	(490,549)	(392,439)
Submarket #5 (10,686,797)	534,339	1,068,679	1,100,700	1,111,436
Submarket #6 (4,229,234)	344,400	340,000	343,219	340,045
Submarket #7 (8,437,266)	337,490	421,863	506,235	590,609
Submarket #8 (1,770,813)	177,081	88,540	89,000	90,874

Absorption data is often available through brokerage houses and may be available through various Internet Listing Services such as CoStar. Appraisers also have access to this information, and many brokers send out regular market data reports to management firms.

However, absorption data can be very difficult to obtain in some local markets. By capturing this data from more than one firm, a manager might be able to compile the data, generate a comprehensive report, and calculate absorption individually.

There are also subscription services that provide absorption information by product type and geography, such as REIS. Often, these services allow the manager to narrow the search to MSA, city, or zip code.

Market Share

The subject property represents a percentage of the total supply in the market area; that percentage is used to determine the building's *market share.* Using that percentage measured against annual absorption for the submarket, you can predict the building's *natural capture rate,* or how long it will take to lease your vacant space.

Subject Square Feet ÷ Total Square Feet = X%

Example:

If there are 2,950,000 square feet of Class C Office Space in the market, and the subject property is 62,500 square feet, the market share is calculated as follows:

62,500 ÷ 2,950,000 = 2.12% Market Share of Total Supply

This percentage can be applied to anticipated absorption to calculate a lease-up velocity. By multiplying a building's market share times the estimated absorption, you calculate *lease-up velocity.* Anticipated deviations from this market share need to be justified and explained.

Example:

Using 150,600 square feet as the absorption

2.12% (market share) × 150,600 = 3,193 sq ft of Anticipated Leasing for One Year

Office Building Feasibility

Absorption is one of many factors considered in deciding whether to construct a new building. There are two approaches to estimating absorption for a particular building:

- Analyze absorption at recently constructed properties that are comparable to the subject building
- Use *capture rate analysis* of competing properties

METHOD	EXAMPLE
Absorption Values at Recent Constructions	• New buildings leased an average of 25,000 square feet per month
Capture Rate Analysis	• Assume that four competing buildings will capture 25% of the market • Divide annual absorption by four to find each building's share

While the capture rate analysis approach is straightforward, consider the following:

- Unequal allocation of building shares may be more appropriate (e.g., one building has superior features)
- The approach does not account for other new office buildings that might be in development state

Using the two approaches together will result in more accurate potential absorption for a single building.

tips

An accurate absorption estimate depends on the unique features of the subject building, the amount of preleasing that can be accomplished, and the ability to negotiate rents to speed the leasing process.

BREAK-EVEN ANALYSIS

The real estate manager must also consider the *break-even point,* or the occupancy rate at which rents are just sufficient to cover expenses and debt service. A *break-even analysis* measures the vulnerability of the property to changes in occupancy.

(Operating Expenses + Annual Debt Service) ÷ Gross Potential Income
= Minimum Break-Even Point

Example:

Consider a property with the following financials:

Gross Potential Income	=	$589,000
Annual Operating Expenses	=	$211,000
Annual Debt Service Payments	=	$290,500

($211,000 + $290,500) ÷ $589,000 = $501,500 ÷ $589,000 = 0.85 = 85%

An *investor's break-even point* covers an additional specified return on the investment. In other words, it calculates the occupancy rate required to earn a certain rate of return.

(Operating Expenses + Annual Debt Service + *Return on Investment*) ÷ Gross Potential Income = Investor's Break-Even Point

PROPERTY ANALYSIS

So far, our analysis has centered on gathering and studying a variety of data regarding the region and neighborhood of the office building. The next component of the analysis is to examine the subject property as well as comparable properties in the market area. Comparable properties are used to identify differences from the subject property for the purposes of estimating market rents.

Key site factors and attributes to consider in a property analysis include:

FACTOR/ATTRIBUTE	DESCRIPTION
Location 	• Most important factor • Well-located office building can command higher rents despite inefficient design or other factors • Well-maintained but poorly located site may not generate income necessary to operate efficiently • Access and convenience important (business support services, restaurants, banks, shopping)
Accessibility 	• Chance of success increased if located on, or close to, a major thoroughfare • Easy accessibility from interchange points between expressways and freeways essential • Access to public transportation and ease and availability of parking important • Ease and safety of entering and exiting (e.g., left turn lanes, deceleration lanes, and so forth) key factors
Tenancy 	• Manager should record the following data: company name, type of business, number of employees, leased square footage, potential expansion, credit history, and so forth • Prospects give careful consideration to the tenancy of a building

FACTOR/ATTRIBUTE	DESCRIPTION

Management

- Prospects will be concerned with how well the property is maintained, whether there are good security and waste disposal services, if public areas are kept clean and well-lighted, the lawn is trimmed, the parking lot pavement smooth, the trash is removed at regular intervals, and so forth

Reference the following checklist for a comprehensive list of site factors/attributes to analyze:

CHECKLIST: SITE FACTORS/ATTRIBUTES

- ☐ Location
- ☐ Accessibility
- ☐ Tenancy
- ☐ Management
- ☐ Age
- ☐ Architectural design and style
- ☐ Physical condition
- ☐ Size, interior space, and public areas and amenities
- ☐ Zoning and land-use restrictions
- ☐ Efficiency (ratio of net rentable area to the usable area [%])
- ☐ Building systems (e.g., HVAC, elevators, technology) condition/age
- ☐ Maintenance and janitorial service
- ☐ Security
- ☐ Grounds, landscaping, and detached structures
- ☐ Parking
- ☐ Availability of public and private utilities
- ☐ Image
- ☐ Floor plates (configuration/shape of leasable space)
- ☐ Green building efficiencies, sustainability

1. Maintenance and janitorial
2. Elevators
3. HVAC
4. Security
5. Management

"Maintenance and service issues reflect on our ability to maintain the property at a competitive level so that it will increase in value over time."

– *Sam Chanin, CPM®, Aliso Viejo, California*

COMPARISON GRID ANALYSIS

After determining the attributes of your subject property, it is time to examine the property in relation to other similar buildings. A comparison may reveal differences in factors such as lease terms, amenities, and curb appeal, which affect the rent a property can command.

Overview

A *comparison grid analysis* is a compilation of data that allows comparison of the rents and features of similar office buildings. It is used to calculate market rents for your building and helps assure that a competitive schedule of rental rates is developed.

Comparison grid analysis is a mixture of art and science. The first challenge is selecting the properties to compare to your subject property. One of the best ways to identify comparable properties is to ask and answer the following questions:

- Where do my tenant prospects shop when they consider my property?
- When tenants move into my property, what property did they vacate?
- When tenants move out of my property, to what property do they move?

Also, consider the following:

- Look for the closest competitor properties
- Choose buildings that are similar to yours in type and size

- Ensure the space available for lease is designed for office use; office space cannot be compared to retail space.
- Compare the subject property to two or more comparable properties whenever possible

Comparison grid analysis is a valuable tool because it focuses attention on the importance and value of different features of the building. However, comparisons are essentially subjective because the choice of features to be compared and the values assigned to them are usually a matter of judgment. The two essential challenges to making valuable comparisons follow:

- Determining which similar features/attributes have a competitive edge and will actually affect rental rates
- Determining the *range of value* to the competitive advantage that one property feature has over similar features of its competitor

To gather relevant facts about the comparables:

- Visit each building and compile a list of its features (e.g., tenants, parking, proximity to transit, overall appearance)
- Research the economics of leases in your market. Focus your research on finding common asking rates for comparable space, and rates at which deals are made once negotiations have begun. Brokers can share terms of recent lease deals in the market without giving the names of the tenants or buildings. It is critical that the deal making rate is obtained or the market survey will not be current.
- Gather vacancy rates on competing properties by networking with other local managers

FIGURE 2-8: COMPARISON GRID?

I Said	You Said

"I don't know why anyone would use a comparison grid. It seems so outdated."	"Reliable information is hard to come by. A smart manager will always want to conduct market research to keep pricing competitive and to understand one's competition. Without a tool like the comp grid, we're only guessing. It really is the only way you can accurately determine market rents."

"But, it is so subjective. How does it really work?"	"It is subjective, but amenities and the value of certain property characteristics can also be subjective. The comparison grid provides an opportunity to assign values and determine a reasonable range for specific line items based on the overall impact on the rental rate. It is up to the manager to make assessments that are thoughtful and realistic. Experience in the marketplace will narrow the possible range of values. Also, collaborating with your leasing team can help you arrive at realistic values. Keep your metrics consistent and the grid will do the rest!"
"What tips do you have for determining the value of features?"	"Know your competition. Understanding major differences can help in assigning a reasonable range of values and determining appropriate rental rate adjustments. Also, a few pennies can go a long way. Keep your value changes small enough to be realistic yet measurable. Remember, be consistent!"

Steps

The steps for conducting a comparison grid analysis are as follows:

1. Describe the subject property

2. Determine the features

3. Describe the comparable properties

4. Determine the value of features

5. Total the value adjustments

6. Analyze the adjusted rents

Next, we will walk through the key steps of building the comparison grid and performing the analysis. The completed office building comparison grid for the property we will use, known as "111 Main St," will be shown after we've reviewed all steps.

Resources:

Downloadable forms such as office building comparison grids can be found on *www.irem.org* and are free for members. These sample forms and agreements are not endorsed by the Institute of Real Estate Management. They are presented for informational purposes only.

❶ Describe the subject property

4		Subject
5	**Property Name**	111 Main
6	Base rental rate	
7	- Concessions	
8	+ Exp. pass-throughs	
9	+ Tenant-paid improv.	
10	= Effective rent	

The information gathered in the property analysis is used to complete the subject portion of the comparison grid analysis. It is helpful to include address information for the subject property.

❷ Determine the features

After the subject property is selected:

- Detail characteristics or features of the property that affect rent
- Include information such as location, age, and market presence
- Select features based on their value to tenants and their value in marketing the property to tenants
- Rate each feature (poor, fair, good, very good, excellent)

12	Categories	Description
13	Location/accessibility	Good
14	Age	17
15	Market presence	Good
16	Building condition:	
17	Exterior	Fair
18	Grounds	Excellent
19	Common areas	Good
20	Office space	Good
21	Other	

❸ Describe the comparable properties

Once the subject property's features are described in the comparison grid:

- Enter property data and features for the comparable properties
- Use the greatest number of comparable properties possible to maximize the effectiveness of the adjusted rent calculation
- Ensure that each of the properties selected is comparable to one another as well as to the subject property
- Visit comparable properties and compile a list of their features
- Evaluate features in comparison to the subject property and rate each feature (poor, fair, good, very good, excellent)

4		Subject	Comparable 1		Comparable 2		Comparable 3	
5	**Property Name**	111 Main	430 West		Grand Tower		22 N Jefferson	
6	Base rental rate		$14.25		$14.00		$10.50	
7	- Concessions		$1.43		$0.00		$0.88	
8	+ Exp. pass-throughs		$0.00		$0.00		$1.35	
9	+ Tenant-paid improv.		$0.40		$0.00		$0.80	
10	= Effective rent		$13.22		$14.00		$11.77	
11								
12	**Categories**	**Description**	**Description**	**+\- Adj**	**Description**	**+\- Adj**	**Description**	**+\- Adj**
13	Location/accessibility	Good	Good		Good		Poor	
14	Age	17	65		12		15	
15	Market presence	Good	Fair		Excellent		Poor	

CHECKLIST: GATHERING INFORMATION

- ☐ Age
- ☐ Market presence
- ☐ Building condition
- ☐ Parking
- ☐ Building systems
- ☐ Available space/vacancies
- ☐ Amenities
- ☐ Economics (e.g., rental rates, concessions, pass-through items)

One of the best ways to gather information is to call and introduce yourself to the building manager, state the type of information you are seeking, and share that kind of information about your property. Other managers are more likely to reciprocate if you share information about your building up front.

tips

Determine the value of features

The next step is to compare the differences between the subject property and the comparables:

- Enter a value in the adjustment column next to each feature indicating what a tenant would pay for each feature or would not pay because of the feature's absence
- Recognize that determining which similar features have the competitive edge, as well as the range of value to the competitive advantage, depends on your judgment and knowledge of the market
  - If the comparable is rated **INFERIOR** to the subject property, assign a **POSITIVE** number to adjust the comparable upward
  - If the comparable is rated **SUPERIOR** to the subject property, assign a **NEGATIVE** number to adjust the comparable downward
- Don't change the subject property, change the comparables

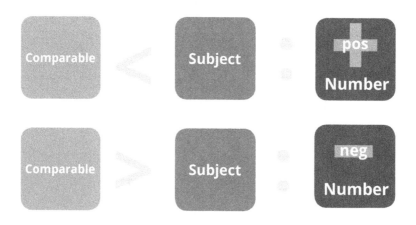

For example, the "elevator" feature at 430 West is rated "Excellent," while the same feature at the subject property is rated "Good." In this case, since the comparable property is superior to the subject property, the adjustment is entered as a negative number.

4		Subject	Comparable 1		Comparable 2		Comparable 3	
5	**Property Name**	111 Main	430 West		Grand Tower		22 N Jefferson	
6	Base rental rate		$14.25		$14.00		$10.50	
7	- Concessions		$1.43		$0.00		$0.88	
8	+ Exp. pass-throughs		$0.00		$0.00		$1.35	
9	+ Tenant-paid improv.		$0.40		$0.00		$0.80	
10	= Effective rent		$13.22		$14.00		$11.77	
11								
12	**Categories**	Description	Description	+\- Adj	Description	+\- Adj	Description	+\- Adj
13	Location/accessibility	Good	Good	$0.00	Good	$0.00	Poor	$0.70
14	Age	17	65	$0.20	12	-$0.35	15	-$0.05
15	Market presence	Good	Fair	$0.15	Excellent	-$0.40	Poor	$0.40

16	Building condition:						
17	Exterior	Fair	Good	-$0.05	Good	-$0.05	Excellent	-$0.10
18	Grounds	Excellent	Good	$0.05	Good	$0.05	Excellent	$0.00
19	Common areas	Good	Excellent	-$0.15	Good	$0.00	Good	$0.00
20	Office space	Good	Good	$0.00	Excellent	-$0.15	Fair	$0.05
21	Other						
22	Building systems:						
23	Elevators	Good	Excellent	-$0.10	Good	$0.00	Poor	$0.10
24	HVAC efficiency	Good	Excellent	-$0.10	Good	$0.00	Fair	$0.10
25	After hours charge	Good	N/A	-$0.05	Good	$0.00	Good	$0.00
26	Life safety	Good	Excellent	-$0.15	Good	$0.00	Good	$0.00

Q&A: Value Adjustments

Q. How do you decide the value to assign to each feature?

A. The general guideline is to consider what a tenant would pay for each feature or would not pay because of the feature's absence. The goal is to determine a value that has an impact, but doesn't skew the effective rent. It is a balance between selecting too low a number that doesn't change the rent enough, and selecting too high a number that changes the rent too much. Personal judgment and knowledge of the market are key.

Q. What if you can't determine a value?

A. In situations in which the estimated value of a feature cannot be determined, make more conservative adjustments to avoid over-adjusting a comparable's rent.

A drawback to one building in effect is an expense that is passed through, while a sought-after amenity can be thought of as a concession (hence, the adjustments are down for desirable features).

tips

 Total the value adjustments

Once you identify the value of each feature:

- Total the adjustments for each property
- Add or subtract the total adjustment from the comparable property's rent to determine the adjusted effective rent

4		Subject	Comparable 1	Comparable 2	Comparable 3
5	**Property Name**	111 Main	430 West	Grand Tower	22 N Jefferson
6	Base rental rate		$14.25	$14.00	$10.50
7	- Concessions		$1.43	$0.00	$0.88
8	+ Exp. pass-throughs		$0.00	$0.00	$1.35
9	+ Tenant-paid improv.		$0.40	$0.00	$0.80
10	= Effective rent		$13.22	$14.00	$11.77
11					
52	Total rent adjustments		$0.35	-$0.70	$0.85
53	Adjusted effective rent		$13.57	$13.30	$12.62

6 Analyze the adjusted rents

To determine the approximate market rent for the subject property, average the adjusted effective rents of the comparable properties.

For this example: **$13.57 + 13.30 + 12.62 = $39.49 ÷ 3 = $13.16**

53	Adjusted effective rent			$13.57	$13.30	$12.62
54	**Average adjusted effective rent**	**$13.16**				

We've just reviewed how to complete a comparison grid analysis for purposes of setting rental rates. In addition, a comparison grid analysis can help you highlight strengths and weaknesses of the subject property relative to the competition.

An evaluation of competing properties should also include an assessment of their tenancies:

- What tenants are already in the market?
- Are the tenants with an established presence looking for additional space?
- What tenants or types of tenants are not represented in the market?

These may be prospects that could enhance your property. Conversely, there may be economic or demographic reasons why these tenants do not have a presence in your market.

SMART PHONE APP

The IREM comps app is a tool that allows you to establish competitive rents for your office building. You can enter data for three comparable properties and the app will calculate the adjusted effective rent for your subject property. You will also have the ability to e-mail the results in spreadsheet format to anyone.

http://itunes.apple.com/app/irem-comps/id399895107?mt=8

SCAN THE QR CODE TO DOWNLOAD THIS APP.

FIGURE 2-9: SAMPLE COMPARISON GRID

#		Subject	Comparable 1		Comparable 2		Comparable 3	
4		**Subject**	**Comparable 1**		**Comparable 2**		**Comparable 3**	
5	**Property Name**	111 Main	430 West		Grand Tower		22 N Jefferson	
6	Base rental rate		$14.25		$14.00		$10.50	
7	- Concessions		$1.43		$0.00		$0.88	
8	+ Exp. pass-throughs		$0.00		$0.00		$1.35	
9	+ Tenant-paid improv.		$0.40		$0.00		$0.80	
10	= Effective rent		$13.22		$14.00		$11.77	
11								
12	**Categories**	**Description**	**Description**	**+/-**	**Description**	**+/-**	**Description**	**+/-**
13	Location/accessibility	Good	Good	$0.00	Good	$0.00	Poor	$0.70
14	Age	17	65	$0.20	12	-$0.35	15	-$0.05
15	Market presence	Good	Fair	$0.15	Excellent	-$0.40	Poor	$0.40
16	Building condition:							
17	Exterior	Fair	Good	-$0.05	Good	-$0.05	Excellent	-$0.10
18	Grounds	Excellent	Good	$0.05	Good	$0.05	Excellent	$0.00
19	Common areas	Good	Excellent	-$0.15	Good	$0.00	Good	$0.00
20	Office space	Good	Good	$0.00	Excellent	-$0.15	Fair	$0.05
21	Other							
22	Building systems:							
23	Elevators	Good	Excellent	-$0.10	Good	$0.00	Poor	$0.10
24	HVAC efficiency	Good	Excellent	-$0.10	Good	$0.00	Fair	$0.10
25	After hours charge	Good	N/A	-$0.05	Good	$0.00	Good	$0.00
26	Life safety	Good	Excellent	-$0.15	Good	$0.00	Good	$0.00
27	Other							
28	Available space:							
29	Location	Floor 11/Good view	F1.7/Good view	$0.55	F1.7/Good view	$0.55	River view	-$0.60
30	Floor plate	16,284 s.f.	15,860 s.f.	$0.00	22,768 s.f.	$0.00	30,000 s.f.	$0.05
31	Window modulation	5 feet	5 feet	$0.00	6 feet	-$0.05	4.5 feet	$0.00
32	Other							
33	Parking:							
34	Type	Garage	N/A	$0.20	Garage	$0.00	Open	$0.10
35	Visitor space	Pay hourly	Public	$0.05	Pay hourly	$0.00	Public	$0.05
36	Cost to tenant	$65/month each	N/A		Free	-$0.15	Free	-$0.15
37								
38								
39								
40	Amenities/features							
41	Bank	Yes	None	$0.05	Yes	$0.00	No	$0.05
42	Security	24-hour guards	24-hour guards	$0.00	24-hour	$0.00	Nights only	$0.10
43	Eating facilities	None	Snack shop	-$0.05	Cafeteria	-$0.05	2 Restaurants	-$0.10
44	Storage	None	Free	-$0.15	None	$0.00	None	$0.00
45	Other retail	None	None	$0.00	Newstand	-$0.05	None	$0.00
46	Temperature control	Zoned by floor	3 zones/floor	-$0.05	Zoned	$0.00	No individual controls	$0.05
47	Proximity to hotels	Average	Close by	-$0.05	Close by	-$0.05	Far away	$0.05
48	Day Care	No	No	$0.00	Yes	-$0.05	No	$0.00
49	Travel Agency	Yes	No	$0.05	No	$0.05	No	$0.05
50	Vacancy Rate	10%	16%	-$0.05	10%	$0.00	10%	$0.00
51								
52	Total rent adjustments			$0.35		-$0.70		$0.85
53	Adjusted effective rent			$13.57		$13.30		$12.62
54	**Average adjusted effective rent**	**$13.16**						

Websites:

www.demographicsnow.com

www.siteselection.com (Site Selection: The Magazine of Corporate Real Estate Strategy & Area Economic Development)

www.stdbonline.com (CCIM Institute Site to Do Business)

www.irem.org/resources/by-topic/marketing--communications (IREM Resources: Marketing & Communications)

CHAPTER 3

Developing Marketing Plans

This book follows the typical timeline of an office building lease deal. The timeline below shows where we are within the process.

Understanding Office Buildings	Assessing the Market	**Developing Marketing Plans**	Developing Leasing Plans	Formulating the Lease	Retaining Tenants

Selecting appropriate marketing strategies and techniques attracts tenants to the building, increases signed leases, increases tenant retention, and maximizes income for the owner. A property manager must be able to determine appropriate marketing strategies, plans, and tactics for the office building.

What's in this chapter:

- Marketing Strategies
- Marketing Plan
- Marketing Tactics
- Measuring Effectiveness

MARKETING STRATEGIES

There is a direct relationship between planning and the success of a property, therefore developing a marketing program should not be taken lightly. The first step is to determine an overall strategy, taking into account the current context of the market.

Current Context

Today's tenants have access to a tremendous amount of information about potential office buildings. Tenants are active participants in the leasing process, and they expect an interactive experience when searching for their new space. Access to the Internet and other technologies allow the tenant to:

- Find available office space
- Tour properties virtually
- Become familiar with pricing
- Review building amenities
- Research various markets
- Monitor market conditions

Now more than ever, first impressions are critical. You may not even realize when a potential tenant is considering your property and narrowing down their short list. In order to draw in prospective tenants and entice them to visit your property in person, a solid marketing approach must be in place.

tips

Despite the plethora of information available, the office building lease deal is a sophisticated transaction. Nothing can replace the value the real estate manager brings to the transaction.

Outside Broker vs. In-House

In order to ensure your property is represented well in the marketplace and increase the possibility of the in-person site visit, you must think strategically about how to market your available space. Do you take on marketing activities in-house with your leasing agents, or hire an outside broker whose chief function is to bring landlords and tenants together and assist in negotiation?

CHECKLIST: FACTORS TO CONSIDER

- ☐ Owner's goals
- ☐ Budget
- ☐ Size of space
- ☐ Complexity
- ☐ Experience and talent in the market
- ☐ Comfort level with third party responsible for brand
- ☐ Desired tenant mix

Selecting a Broker

The next step is to select the right broker for the job.

CHECKLIST: SELECTING THE RIGHT BROKER

- ☐ Reputation (Regionally strong? Nationally strong? Strong because of brand name or because of person?)
- ☐ Previous experience
- ☐ Proven abilities
- ☐ Specialty or focus area
- ☐ Knowledge of market
- ☐ Size of team
- ☐ Responsibilities of team members (e.g., who does cold calling?)
- ☐ Resources of brokerage house
- ☐ Type of building
- ☐ Competing and/or complementary listings

Working with Cooperating Brokers

The real estate brokerage community is a critical part of the successful lease-up of commercial properties. Be sure to maintain and enhance this relationship on an ongoing basis to maximize potential for filling your space in an effective and efficient manner.

Dos and Don'ts: Working with Brokers

DO Ensure that owner's and tenant's representatives (brokers) speak the same language.

DON'T Forget to keep ownership informed of all developments.

DO Hold regular meetings.

DON'T Let brokerage fees get caught up in a lengthy accounting process. You don't want a reputation of slow payment, or you won't get the deals.

DO Respond promptly to all broker inquiries to facilitate more showings and ultimately more leases.

DON'T Wait to start marketing available space.

DO Stay in touch with brokers through open houses, personal communication, and other events. This helps them get to know your property and allows you to provide information on potential space availability, rates, and so forth.

DON'T Forget that the goal is to close deals. Make sure you protect the broker's position in the deal. Recognize that both parties may have to negotiate on commission (especially during tough economic times).

DO Know your state licensing laws.

DON'T Hesitate to get creative (e.g., some owners provide free DRE courses for brokers to renew licenses).

DO Use a comprehensive broker's agreement that stipulates the following points: weekly status report of activity, registration of broker's clients, broker leasing commissions and how they are calculated.

Types of Broker Listings

Brokers can have one of two types of listing arrangements with the owner or developer of a particular building.

LISTING TYPE	DESCRIPTION
Exclusive 	• Broker assured in writing that the owner will not deal with any other leasing agent without paying a fee to the original broker. • Broker is guaranteed a commission if the deal is closed, no matter who brought the tenant to the owner.
Nonexclusive (open) 	• Gives the owner the right to deal with other agents. • If the original broker actually closes the deal, he or she gets paid a commission. If not, the owner is not required to pay the original broker any fee. • Some owners believe this gives them more freedom (not locked in to the performance of a single broker). • Some brokers will refuse to work on a nonexclusive basis.

BROKER COMMISSION AGREEMENTS

The leasing commission is usually paid by the property owner, and the amount of commission and time at which it is paid are both fully negotiable. However, keep in mind that above-market commissions may attract brokers, while below-market commissions may deter brokers. Market leaders, defined by portfolio size or higher quality properties, may define the market commission rate. Commission terms should be set by the owner and should be stated in the property's management agreement. It is important to know and understand your negotiating position.

Many variations exist on how and when the broker should be paid, therefore it is important to specify the terms. For example:

- Paid up front
- Paid 50% of the commission when the lease is signed and 50% after the tenant has moved in
- Declining percent commissions (calculated in declining installments over lease term)
- Split commissions (payment divided among two or more brokers)

tips

Regardless of listing type, the agreement should be put in writing and signed by all parties.

A commission agreement should always be signed to legally bind all parties.

tips

To draw up commission agreements that serve the owner's interests and avoid unnecessary fees, structure your approach to commissions using the following points:

- Define that commissions will be paid on base rent only and will not include expense reimbursements and other pass through payments, and that base rent will be offset by all rent concessions.
- Exclude base rent increases such as escalations. Do not include percentage rent (retail), utility payments, or lease buy-outs.
- Do not include lease options to expand or renew when agreeing to lease terms. Restrict the scope and term of the lease. Do not include short-term leases with renewal options or options to expand. Short-term leases with renewal options favor the broker with opportunities for repeated commissions, in addition to limiting the landlord's flexibility to market the space to prospective tenants.

FLAT PERCENT

In the case of a *flat percent commission* for long-term leases, the broker is paid a fee based on the rent over the term of the lease multiplied by a negotiated percentage rate. *Gross rent* represents the aggregate rent for the entire term of the tenant's lease.

Leased Sq Ft × Rent Rate × Length of Lease = Gross Rent
Gross Rent × % Rate = Commission

Example:

Let's say a tenant signs a three-year lease for a 1,800 square foot office at $15 per square foot per year. The broker's negotiated flat rate is 5%.

1,800 sq ft × $15/sq ft/yr. × 3 years = $81,000 Gross Rent

$81,000 × .05 = $4,050 Commission

DOLLARS PER SQUARE FOOT

With a *dollars per square foot commission,* an agreed-upon rate is multiplied by the total square footage of the space.

Leased Sq Ft × Rate = Commission

If, in the case of our 1,800 square foot office, the broker was paid $3 per square foot, the broker would make a $5,400 commission.

1,800 sq ft × $3/sq ft = $5,400

DECLINING PERCENT (SLIDING SCALE)

Declining percent commission (also known as *sliding scale* commissions) involves the broker being paid at a declining rate over the course of the lease term. The percentage rate is decreased as the term progresses, and the rate and payment schedule are negotiable.

Let's say the broker is paid according to the following schedule:

- 6% for first 12 months
- 3% for next 12 months
- 2% for remainder of the term

1,800 sq ft × $15/sq ft/yr = $27,000 Rent per Year

Year 1: $27,000 × .06 = $1,620   Commission
Year 2: $27,000 × .03 = $810   Commission
Year 3: $27,000 × .02 = $540   Commission

$1,620 + $810 + $540 = $2,970   Commission

ENGAGING THE BROKER COMMUNITY

If brokers aren't looking at your marketing pieces, they have no idea why your space is better than the next. Particularly in economic markets, it isn't just the space that must be competitive. Broker commissions and bonuses are critical.

If you use any special broker incentives, specify them. Know tax implications, real estate licensing laws, and the brokerage firm's policy on incentives. Examples of incentives might be:

- Gifts for bringing a prospect to the property for a showing
- Vacation trips for attracting a full-floor tenant
- Cash bonuses for brokers who register the greatest number of acceptable prospects for the building
- An automobile for a broker who makes the largest deal with a large credit tenant acceptable to the building
- Giveaways for tours over x amount of square feet
- Transwestern's campaign where the broker who accumulated the most points

at the end of the year won $10,000. Brokers earned points by signing leases, conducting property tours, and being the first to correctly answer a monthly e-blast trivia question (questions were designed to draw brokers to the website or brochure for the answer)

- Stream Realty's airline miles giveaway program (refer to Figure 3-1)
- Transwestern's boarding pass program (refer to Figure 3-2)

FIGURE 3-1: ENGAGING THE BROKER COMMUNITY SAMPLE 1

STREAM REALTY

ABOUT STREAM | PEOPLE | PROPERTY SEARCH | LOCATIONS | SERVICES | PRINCIPAL TRANSACTIONS | MEDIA

Home >> SRP Blog

People Finder
Leadership
In the Community

STREAM OC LAUNCHES MILES FOR TOURS PROGRAM

By Stream Realty Partners, L.P.

Monday, June 04, 2012 6:00 AM

Stream Orange County recently kicked off its "Miles for Tours" program, which encourages and rewards tenant rep brokers for touring select Stream properties with their prospective tenants. The program is built around a partnership with Delta Airline's Skymiles program and rewards brokers with one mile for every five square feet of space toured.

Participating properties in Orange County include:

- Summit Office Campus, a prime corporate location
- Highpointe in Mission Viejo, a premier Class "A" office building
- 101 Pacifica, a prestigious jewel box building
- Highpark Center, the best value in South County
- the best location in Corporate Park

Source: Enis Hartz, CPM®

FIGURE 3-2: ENGAGING THE BROKER COMMUNITY SAMPLE 2

Source: Enis Hartz, CPM®

MARKETING PLAN

Two types of plans are commonly used when leasing office space:

- The **MARKETING PLAN** is used to advertise and relay information about the property for the purposes of attracting prospective tenants to the property (macro plan that provides marketing vision and goals)
- The **LEASING PLAN,** on the other hand, can be considered a component of the broader, overall marketing plan and is intended to identify specific spaces within the building that are to be leased

For the remainder of this chapter, we will focus on the components and functions of the marketing plan; the leasing plan will be discussed further in the next Chapter.

Marketing Plan Overview

Your marketing plan (and your leasing plan) should be developed to meet the owner's goals and objectives. For example:

- A short-term hold may indicate that the owner is speculating in the real estate market, which might generate an emphasis on the need to quickly increase the property's occupancy. This in turn could raise the value of the property, which the owner will realize as a profit on the sale of the property.
- A short-term hold may result in the following:
  - A focus on gaining occupancy quickly with minimum capital investment in tenant improvements
  - Rent structures may focus on lower rental rates and fewer tenant improvement (TI) contributions
  - Placement of tenants within the building may not be managed to accommodate future growth
- Long-term holds may indicate that the owner is investing, rather than speculating, in the real estate market. Investment in real estate offers investors five fundamental opportunities:
  1. Periodic return, or cash flow
  2. Capital preservation
  3. Capital appreciation
  4. Leverage
  5. Income tax advantages
- A long-term hold may result in the following:
  - Owners may be more concerned about the quality of tenants in the building, and therefore, may be more selective in screening prospects
  - Rental rates and terms may reflect a willingness on the part of the owner to contribute to tenant improvements
  - The future expansion needs of tenants may be considered when placing tenants within the building
- An owner of a property whose goal is capital preservation may allocate some funds from the marketing plan into capital improvements, because owners

looking for long-term appreciation often invest the most money to attract the best tenants.

- The owner's objectives may also be driven by cash flow needs. How you treat cash flow will determine the amount of funds available for marketing.

Marketing Plan Components

After assessing the market in which the property is located, it is time to develop a plan for attracting tenants to the office building.

COMPONENT	DESCRIPTION
Purpose	• Drives marketing plan and attempts to identify how much space needs to be leased and how fast. • Reflects owner's goals and objectives. • Should have SMART goals (refer to Figure 3-3).
Target Market	• Segment of the overall market for which the property is likely to be appealing. • Based on market assessment. • Narrows your search for tenants. Can target based on industry, tenants who do similar work to those in nearby buildings, building type, and so forth. • Affected by size and configuration of the building's floor plate as well as location. • May reflect those who are not in the market but should be.
Key Messages	• Vary based on importance to prospect. • Should position the property for competitive advantage. • Promote features of the property that set it apart from competitors (e.g., lower rental rates, better location, reputation, service). • Ensure appropriate brand and theme: • **BRAND:** Overall concept created to reflect a "feel" or "perception" that your property creates. Promoted in messaging by a name, symbol, design, fonts, color scheme, and so forth. It is a visual strategy on how the property fits the needs of the target market. • **THEME:** Images, ideas, or symbols that are used to convey either a time-based message that can be adjusted (e.g., seasonal themes) or a specific promotion of part of the property.
Timetable	• Establishes a schedule for planning, production, and release of marketing tactics (refer to Figure 3-4).
Budget	• Specifies money allocated for each activity that is related to marketing the property (refer to Checklist). • Details variation in costs based on owner's goals and other considerations (e.g., new building).

FIGURE 3-3: SMART GOALS

- The acronym **SMART** was introduced by Peter Drucker's 1957 publication, "The Practice of Management," and refers to:
  - **S**pecific,
  - **M**easurable,
  - **A**greed Upon,
  - **R**ealistic, and
  - **T**ime-Based goals
- *Specific* means that the goal should be precise and explicit, not general or broad. For example, a general goal for the property would be "To acquire more tenants." A specific goal might be "To achieve 90% occupancy by December 31."
- The purpose of your plan should be ***Measurable***, and the more specific it is, the easier it will be to quantify results.
- The purpose of the plan should be ***Agreed*** upon by all parties. Using the owner's objectives as a foundation, gain buy-in from all leasing staff on the marketing and leasing goals for the building.
- The purpose should be ***Realistic***; increasing occupancy by 20% in two months may not be an attainable goal for the building. To be realistic, the goal must be one that you are both ***willing*** and ***able*** to achieve.
- The goal should always be ***Time-based.*** Set a specific deadline for completion of the goal. "To decrease vacancy rate by 4% within six months" or "To lease Suite C23 by January 31" would be effective time-based goals.

FIGURE 3-4: SAMPLE TIME TABLE

Event	Timing	Comments
Direct mailing of brochures	Nov. 2	
Property Showcase / Broker Open House	Dec. 11	Distribute property promo flyers at the building 12/1–12/10
Vacancy listing on *www.loopnet.com*	Runs throughout the listing period	Add link to *www.loopnet. com* on property website
Site visit: ABC Building	Jan. 15	
E-mail flyers to real estate brokers	Ongoing	

MARKETING BUDGET CONSIDERATIONS

After identifying the goals of a marketing plan, it is time to establish your marketing budget. When determining your budget, consider one of the following methods:

METHOD	DESCRIPTION
Objectives	• Estimates marketing costs to achieve specific marketing objectives • Essential for lease-up scenarios, but can be used in other situations
Percentage	• Established as a percentage of some past effective gross income or future gross potential income • Manager is dependent on good industry benchmarks to set the percentage
Competitive	• Sets marketing expenditures based on what the property's competition is doing • Can be effective when marketing conditions are stable, but it may ignore your property's competitive strengths
Affordable	• Some landlords defer to what they can afford, and marketing is funded after all other expenses • While this might be good cost control, it ignores the property's marketing needs

CHECKLIST: SAMPLE MARKETING PLAN BUDGET COSTS

- ☐ Internet Listing Sites
- ☐ Company/property websites and social media
- ☐ Google adwords and search engine optimization (SEO)
- ☐ Display advertising
- ☐ Signage
- ☐ Print advertisements
- ☐ Production of brochures, letterhead, forms, business cards, floor plans, and so forth
- ☐ Direct marketing
- ☐ Public relations events
- ☐ Brokers
- ☐ Broker open house events
- ☐ Leasing staff
- ☐ Tenant retention

MARKETING TACTICS

In order to attract prospective tenants to new or existing office space, the space as a whole must be promoted. Always keep in mind the owner's goals for the property and the desired return on investment (ROI).

Internet Listing Sites

Commercial listing sites are one of the primary tactics for marketing available office space. The following table provides an overview of the key sites available and their features.

LISTING SITE	DESCRIPTION
	• National online source of commercial real estate information and listings • Provides a robust reporting and research function to make market comparisons more meaningful • Contains powerful data mining and analytical tools with data such as GIS, historical transactions, and tenant information • This is a *verified listing service,* meaning CoStar employees actually phone verify the listings to make certain they are accurate and current
	• National online commercial real estate listing service • Widely used with a large database of properties • Often attracts small to moderate size business owners, including non-institutional owners, performs property searches with limited broker involvement
	• More localized commercial real estate network and listing service that connects owners, brokers, tenants, and investors
 	• Examples of broker-specific databases such as CB Richard Ellis or Transwestern
	• Best for small spaces (e.g., under 2,000 square feet), and targets specific cities, small tenants, and young entrepreneurs • Don't need to engage broker

Property listings on these listing sites should include the following:

- Photographs
- Virtual tours
- Detailed property information
- Leasing contact information

Listing space on these websites is relatively inexpensive and reaches a wide audience. For an additional charge, some sites offer the ability to promote your property as a "featured listing" on the homepage and other high profile areas of the website.

Also, note that each website varies in terms of its unique business structure. Some sites charge to search, but not to list. Others charge to list, but not to search.

FIGURE 3-5: SAMPLE LISTING SITES

Source: www.costar.com

Source: www.cityfeet.com

Additional Advertising Initiatives

In addition to commercial listing sites, the following table provides other advertising outlets, or paid forms of presentation and promotion of the property. Specific outlets will be chosen based on the target market and positioning for competitive advantage.

TYPE	DESCRIPTION
Property website (Figure 3-6)	• Includes building description, available space, photographs, floor plans, social media feeds, leasing contact information, and so forth (refer to checklist below) • Entails determining an appropriate project and website name to avoid confusion or complexity. The value (or hindrances) of names tied to ownership or location indicators should be considered. • May have a mobile version of the website
Search engine optimization (SEO)	• Considers how prospects search for space and seeks to improve the ranking of the property website in the search engine results page the prospect sees • Seeking higher search engine results means more visibility for the property • May be contracted to a vendor that specializes in SEO techniques as part of a coordinated search marketing campaign • Should have analytics set up for the website owner to track improvements in ranking and source of hits • May include both search engine buys (see "adwords" below) and "display network" buys (see "display advertising" below)
Real estate management company website (Figure 3-7)	• Can index all the available space under management • May provide a link from the company website to commercial listing sites as an alternative to posting property listings • Includes company information, searchable property listings, featured properties, and contact information • May have a mobile version of the website
Adwords (Google) (Figure 3-8)	• Places a link and a short description of the link target on a Google search results page • Also known as "sponsored links," which are separate from the search results, these links can advertise your property with one or two sentences and a link to the property website. • Includes "pay-per-click" and display advertising • May be adjusted to only run in searches that are initiated in your specific market

TYPE	DESCRIPTION
Display advertising **(Figures 3-9 and 3-10)**	• Ranges from large or small ads for your property placed on another Web or mobile page—ad sizes and position on page will vary • Entails finding the websites likely to be viewed by your target market to advertise • May include still images or rich media (e.g., video, Flash animation) embedded in a display ad that will not "activate" unless a website user selects the image area.
Classified advertising **(Figure 3-11)**	• Includes classified ads for local print newspapers, magazines, and trade journals, as well as their associated websites • Consists of smaller ads that are relatively inexpensive and have a standardized type and layout • Can appear daily or weekly for newspapers, and per issue for magazines and journals
Print display **(Figure 3-12)**	• Offers a range of opportunity in display ad size and color; larger image and graphic space afford the opportunity to convey property brand, theme, or competitive advantage message; more expensive • Often used for newly developed or renovated properties during initial lease-up or with many available spaces
Collateral materials	• Includes brochures, flyers, and portfolios that are passed out to prospective tenants, available for download on websites, or included in a direct marketing campaign • Should be more general and timeless and maintain consistency with the property's image and theme
Other forms of advertising	• Billboards, broadcast media (television and radio), and direct marketing such as direct mailings and e-mail broadcasts • Follow anti-spam legislation for broadcast e-mails (refer to legal issue on page 79)

CHECKLIST: PROPERTY WEBSITE FEATURES

- ☐ Building description
- ☐ Available space
- ☐ Photographs
- ☐ Virtual tours
- ☐ Prominent tenants
- ☐ Directions and maps
- ☐ Leasing details
- ☐ Floor plans
- ☐ Contact information
- ☐ Site map of the website
- ☐ Social media feeds
- ☐ May have a mobile version of the website

FIGURE 3-6: SAMPLE PROPERTY WEBSITE

Source: www.733tenth.com

Review the website periodically for outdated information that can diminish the site's effectiveness, such as:

tips

- Tenant move-ins/move-outs
- Tenant improvements to suites
- Advertising space that has leased
- Advertising "upcoming or current events" for an expired period

---

FIGURE 3-7: SAMPLE REAL ESTATE MANAGEMENT WEBSITE

Source: www.charlesdunn.com

FIGURE 3-8: SAMPLE AD WORDS

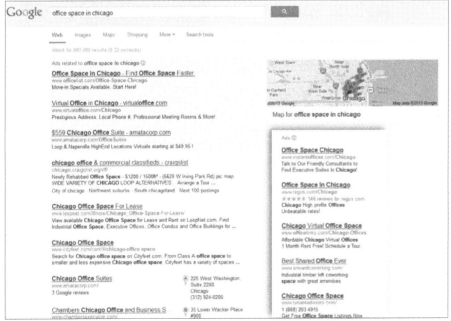

Source: www.google.com

FIGURE 3-9: SAMPLE DISPLAY AD 1

Delivering today's top stories, buzz, commentary ...
Throughout the day, watch the NEW GlobeSt.com for updates.

Connect With Us [f] [y] [in]   Mobile Site [□]

TODAY'S TOP STORIES

GlobeSt Poll, Industry Pros Agree on '13

NEW YORK CITY-No matter how you approach it, the coming year will be a study in slow growth. Read More at GlobeSt.com

Apt. Block Moves for $116M

BERLIN-One of Europe's largest asset managers snaps up 1,384 units here. The buy was made for one of the firm's institutional funds.

Read More

Canadian Buyer Pays $30M for Two Office Buildings

PHOENIX-The buyer acquired an 87,000-SF building on Baseline Road, as well as a 91,000-SF building near Cooper Road and Loop 202 in Chandler, AZ.

Read More

National AM Alert is sponsored by Transwestern and Appraisal Institute.

GLOBAL boutique

Discover our global real estate expertise and local turf knowledge.

⊡ TRANSWESTERN

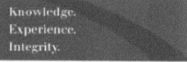

Knowledge.
Experience.
Integrity.

MAI. SRPA. SRA.

The designated difference
behind a name you
can trust.

Appraisal

Source: Enis Hartz, CPM®

76

FIGURE 3-10: SAMPLE DISPLAY AD 2

Source: Enis Hartz, CPM®

FIGURE 3-11: SAMPLE CLASSIFIED ADS

Randhurst Park

$25 psf. Great Office Opportunity!

Located at Hwy 152 East in China Grove.

ABC Office Management

Call (704)555-5555

www.abcmanagement.com

FIGURE 3-12: SAMPLE PRINT DISPLAY ADS

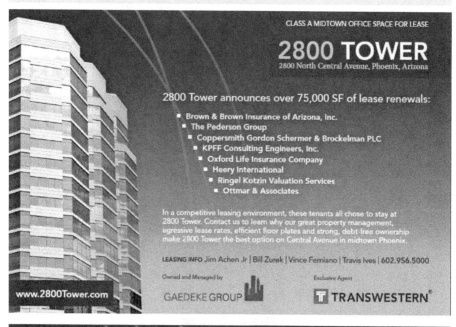

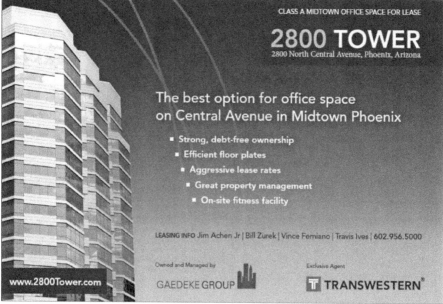

Source: Enis Hartz, CPM®

CHECKLIST: WRITING AN AD

- ☐ Grab the prospect's attention with a sharp graphic or headline
- ☐ Maintain consistency with the property's image and theme
- ☐ Communicate appealing features and competitive advantages and place them in a prominent position
- ☐ Base message on assessment of the target market
- ☐ Remember photographs are more convincing than drawn illustrations
- ☐ Provide information such as property name, address, phone number, website, site plans, square footage, typical office configuration, amenities, services, and prominent tenants
- ☐ Include information about neighborhood features, such as shopping, restaurants, and entertainment venues
- ☐ Use an active voice vs. a passive voice (e.g., "The building features high-tech telecommunications wiring" is more desirable than "There is high-tech telecommunications wiring")
- ☐ End with a "call to action" that prompts the reader to respond by calling or visiting the property (include contact information)

Anti-Spam Legislation. While the possibility of reaching many prospects with very little cost is always tempting, commercial real estate managers must abide by the law. Legislation from 2003 controls unsolicited commercial e-mails. The measure was sought by marketers, retailers, and Internet account providers seeking a single set of rules that would apply nationwide. Requirements that senders of commercial e-mails must follow:

Legal Issue

- Include a legitimate return e-mail and physical postal address
- Include a functioning opt-out mechanism; include clear and conspicuous notice of the opportunity to opt-out; and honor any such opt-out request
- Include a clear and conspicuous notice that the message is an advertisement or solicitation
- Clearly identify messages with pornographic or sexual content as such

In addition, senders are prohibited from falsifying or disguising their true identity and cannot use incorrect, misleading, or fraudulent subject lines.

Q. What about social media? How is it used for marketing and leasing office buildings?

A. Since social media tends to be more of a "peer to peer" networking strategy, it is a tactic more often used in residential property marketing. However, it has some applications to office buildings, such as:

- Promoting events or services provided to tenants (e.g., summer concert series sponsored by building)
- Setting up a Facebook page to promote events in the area such as art fairs, 5K races, and so forth
- Special use properties (e.g., properties near courthouses generally have a high occupancy of attorneys and can have a high degree of "peer to peer" networking due to their need for complementary services such as notary and recording services)
- Note that broker rating sites or commercial rating sites may evolve on which tenants are able to rate office buildings in terms of rates, maintenance, and so forth

Signage

In general, the following signs are applicable to office buildings:

TYPE	DESCRIPTION
For Lease	• Indicate available space and provide leasing contact information • Signs are usually placed inside vacant spaces or at key entrances • Key strategy in marketing vacant space
Identification	• Establish the character of the property and display the name of the building • Typically located at the entrance
Directional	• Direct prospects to the property, visitor parking, and leasing office (if applicable) • Usually include arrows and other directional symbols
Informational	• Provide general information such as hours of operation
Project	• Introduce a site prior to and during construction and may include a rendering of the building, square footage, availability date, names of developers, and leasing contact information

Public Relations

Unlike advertising, *public relations* (PR), refers to any form of promotion that is not paid for, such as press releases and word-of-mouth endorsement. PR is intended to increase awareness and build the image of the property. Clearly, creative public relations can affect your target market at a fraction of the cost of advertising. In fact, some experts say that consumers are five times more likely to be influenced by editorial copy than by advertising. Advertising may be viewed as what you say about your property, while public relations may be viewed as what others say about your property.

PRESS RELEASES

Press releases can be sent to the business or real estate editors of local newspapers as well as broadcast media outlets:

- Develop a relationship with the real estate editor of your local newspaper
- Announce events (e.g., grand opening, community event, changes in management, signing of a major tenant)
- Include relevant information (who, what, when, where, and why)
- Keep short and always include contact information
- Use photographs whenever possible

SPECIAL EVENTS

Special events such as workshops, charity events, or art collection displays at the site generate attention to the property. One could host a myriad of special events at an office building—be creative and research the types of events held by other buildings in the country.

NETWORKING

Networking, or making use of business and professional contacts, is important. Local real estate boards, associations, and financial institutions, even service organizations like the Rotary Clubs are interested in commercial projects and their impact on the local economy. Working with the community on committees and planning boards offers a way to develop business contacts directly.

Socializing with business contacts can help build clientele and expedite leasing. Not every form of entertainment will be suitable for every prospect; however personal preferences should be taken into account.

You should also maintain social contacts with other real estate professionals and leasing agents who can provide referrals. Membership and active participation in professional organizations enhances skills and credentials while providing professional and social interaction with these professionals. Attending annual conferences and participating on committees and boards are other ways to increase this interaction. Organizations that focus on development, leasing, and management of office real estate include:

- Institute of Real Estate Management (IREM)
- Building Owners and Managers Association (BOMA)
- National Association of Industrial and Office Properties (NAIOP)
- Certified Commercial Investment Member (CCIM)

Canvassing and Cold Calling

Direct contact with prospects is called *canvassing* or *cold calling*.

TECHNIQUE	DESCRIPTION
Canvassing 	• Throws a wide net over a geographic area, and can be done face-to-face or over the phone • Goal is to gain access to key decision-makers to acquire information about lease expiration dates, expansion plans, and competitive sites while making prospect aware of available space • Often time-consuming and may not produce immediate results; rejection is common • Expands network of contacts and helps qualify prospects for future listings • Takes practice and experience
Cold Calling 	• Identifying a specific target audience (e.g., lawyers) and calling them • Purpose is to determine if the prospect is interested in space and to arrange a personal interview at another time • Must learn as much as possible about the prospect's business, space requirements, and financial status

CHECKLIST: CANVASSING / COLD CALLING

- ☐ How long have you been at this location?
- ☐ Where were you located prior to this location?
- ☐ How many employees work at this location?
- ☐ Approximately how much space do you occupy?
- ☐ When does your current lease expire? Are there extension options?
- ☐ What do you like and dislike about your current building?
- ☐ In the future, are you more likely to need more space, less space, or about the same amount of space?
- ☐ What specific features or amenities are you/your company looking for?
- ☐ What are you looking for in a neighborhood/surrounding area?

FIGURE 3-13: WHAT TO DO FIRST?

I Said

You Said

"The first thing I do when vacant space becomes available in my building is to work with the broker to list the property on one of the national commercial listing sites."

"I agree that listing sites are essential, especially in our highly technological world. But, I would work with the broker on low-cost, high-impact, high-visibility strategies first and put up a sign."

Case Study: Marketing Tactics

As soon as I have space available in my office parks, I contact the listing broker. I expect him or her to put up a sign and begin an advertising campaign consisting of e-mail blasts, mailings of flyers, and cold calling at a minimum. If I'm not using a broker, I make sure to put up a sign and list the property on commercial real estate listing sites immediately. Then I send out marketing blasts to my current tenants based on what I know about them.

For example, if they are growing, shrinking, have a specific need/use or want to move to another building or park within the portfolio. I even communicate with the tenants I know aren't interested in order to let them know operationally what we're doing and perhaps gain some market intelligence. Offering specials, referral fees, or half month's rent are great ways to generate tenant referrals.

**Sam Chanin, CPM
Aliso Viejo, CA**

MEASURING EFFECTIVENESS

It is critical that you review your leasing results as compared to the cost of marketing to measure the effectiveness of your marketing efforts. Measuring effectiveness is also important in order to hold the broker accountable. In general, the owner wants to know:

- Broker's effort (Brokers can guarantee effort, not results.)
- Leasing activity
- Completed transactions (Owners should track where lost deals go and question brokers why prospects were lost. This analysis often leads to price reductions, rent concessions, or suggestions to make the building more competitive.)

A variety of tools can be used to monitor and record the success of your marketing efforts and track broker progress:

TOOL	DESCRIPTION
Prospect Report	• Logs each prospect contacted about leasing space and additional points of contact with that prospect (phone calls, e-mails, visits, letters of intent, and leases out for signatures) • Is summary of prospect card information
Internal Marketing Report	• Records the frequency of advertising (print ads, direct mailings, billboards, broadcast ads, Internet ads) public relations events, and canvassing • Can report effectiveness of techniques by logging how prospects heard about the property and areas in need of modification
Marketing Activity Report	• Keeps the client informed of leasing activity such as active prospects, submitted proposals, and signed leases • May include charts comparing actual leasing progress to projected activity
Pipeline Report	• Brokers should keep owners aware of new or large competing space coming on the market • This new inventory can change and severely impact market absorption, and owners need to analyze this information and reposition the property accordingly • Also used as a list of prospects.

Advanced Marketing/Advertising Analytics

Statistical analysis of marketing and advertising campaigns, while difficult to initiate, is the best way to track the success of these efforts so that you can determine a precise return on investment, especially for digital marketing. The goal of these solutions is to track and report on leads from every traffic source, revealing which lead channels work best.

CHAPTER 3:
Resources

Websites:

www.irem.org/resources/by-topic/marketing-- communications
(IREM Resources: Marketing & Communications)

CHAPTER 4:

Developing Leasing Plans

This book follows the typical timeline of an office building lease deal. The timeline below shows where we are within the process.

Understanding Office Buildings | Assessing the Market | Developing Marketing Plans | **Developing Leasing Plans** | Formulating the Lease | Retaining Tenants

The real estate manager's leasing strategies and techniques, which maximize rentable space and synergize tenancy, directly impact the success of the office building. A property manager must be able to establish effective leasing plans, tenant mix and placement strategies, space planning techniques, and prospect qualification criteria.

What's in this chapter:

- Leasing Plan
- Tenant Mix and Placement
- Space Planning
- Qualifying Prospects

LEASING PLAN

Once you are attracting prospective tenants to the property with your marketing plan, it is necessary to develop an outline for leasing and for placing the tenants that will create the best synergy at the property. Just as with the marketing plan, the *leasing plan* should always reflect the goals and objectives of the owner.

Overview

The in-house leasing plan typically includes a *stacking plan* of the property, preferably drawn to scale, displaying placement and square footage dimensions of all spaces and the building as a whole. In addition, the leasing plan suggests what types of tenants would be better suited for the office space, based on what the market analysis has shown to generate the best possible mix, and therefore the most income, for the property. The rent schedule portion of the leasing plan outlines the current or desired rents for each space; it may include additional lease terms (extension options, rights of refusal, and so forth), and a *rollover schedule,* which shows lease expiration dates.

Components

The following checklist details information that should be included in the leasing plan:

CHECKLIST: LEASING PLAN COMPONENTS

☐ Stacking plan and details of leasing the space such as:
  ☐ Square footage
  ☐ Rental rates
  ☐ Tenant mix and placement (floor plates)
☐ Rent schedule (current and desired rents) and rollover schedule
☐ Tenant improvement expenses
☐ Tenant renewal possibilities
☐ Cost to renew, taking into account tenant improvements, concessions, and rental rate increases or decreases
☐ Options, expansion rights, tenants not renewing

If the leasing plan is created for an existing building, it may:

- Include recommendations for relocating tenants or changing tenant mix in order to:
  - Respond to changes in the market
  - Increase profits for the building as a whole
  - Create synergies
- Suggest renewals for tenants whose leases expire shortly
- Recommend which leases have potential for renegotiating to achieve a higher desired rent for the space

FIGURE 4-1: SAMPLE STACKING PLAN

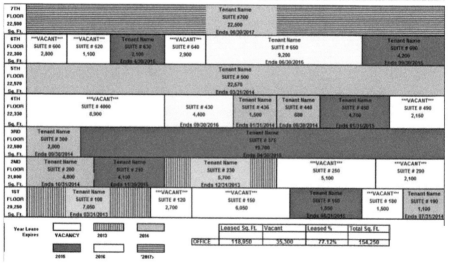

tips

Stacking plans can be formatted specifically for mobile devices. Also, stacking plans in a portable document format (PDF) are usually Smartphone compatible and can be reviewed using the zoom function.

FIGURE 4-2: SAMPLE STACKING PLAN CONT.

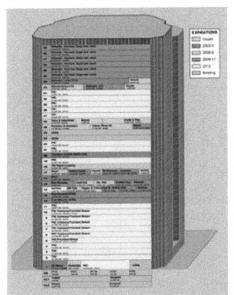

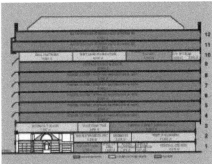

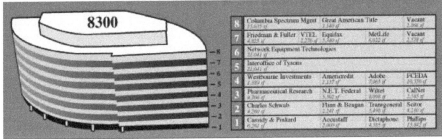

Source: www.replans.com/stacking.html

FIGURE 4-3: SAMPLE ROLLOVER SCHEDULE

ACME OFFICE BUILDING										Preparer:	
Cincinnati, Ohio										Date:	
ROLLOVER											
November 30, 2011											

Floor	Tenant	RSF Leased	% Bldg	Current Term	Expire Date	Annual Base Rent at Expiration	$/rsf /yr	Expense Stop	Opt/ R of R	Opt Ntc Date
120	VACANT	2,707	1.7%							
150	VACANT	6,020	3.9%							
180	VACANT	1,503	1.0%							
250	VACANT	5,130	3.3%							
290	VACANT	2,090	1.3%							
400	VACANT	8,933	5.8%							
430	VACANT	4,458	2.9%							
490	VACANT	2,150	1.4%							
600	VACANT	2,857	1.8%							
620	VACANT	1,143	0.7%							
640	VACANT	2,961	1.9%							
TOTAL VACANT		**39,952**	**25.8%**							
100	Tenant 100	7,042	4.5%		03/31/13					
200	Tenant 200	4,832	3.1%		10/31/13					
230	Tenant 230	5,767	3.7%		12/31/13					
TOTAL EXPIRING 2012		**17,641**	**11.4%**							
436	Tenant 436	1,557	1.0%		01/31/14					
460	Tenant 460	4,786	3.1%		01/31/14					
500	Tenant 500	22,570	14.6%		03/31/14					
440	Tenant 440	681	0.4%		06/30/14					
190	Tenant 190	1,103	0.7%		07/31/14					
300	Tenant 300	2,844	1.8%		09/30/14					
TOTAL EXPIRING 2013		**33,541**	**21.6%**							
160	Tenant 160	1,822	1.2%		03/31/15					
375	Tenant 375	19,764	12.7%		04/30/15					
630	Tenant 630	2,105	1.4%		04/30/15					
690	Tenant 690	4,208	2.7%		09/30/15					
210	Tenant 210	4,161	2.7%		11/30/15					
TOTAL EXPIRING 2014		**32,060**	**20.7%**							
650	Tenant 650	9,296	6.0%		06/30/16					
TOTAL EXPIRING 2015		**9,296**	**6.0%**							
700	Tenant 700	22,535	14.5%		06/30/17					
TOTAL EXPIRING 2016		**22,535**	**14.5%**							
TOTALS		**155,025**	**100.0%**							

FIGURE 4-4: SAMPLE ROLLOVER SCHEDULE

Suite	Tenant	RSF Leased	RSF Vacant	Lease Type	Term (yrs)	Start Date	Expire Date	Annual Base Rent	$/rsf /yr	Rent Inc Date	$/rsf /yr	% Bldg	Exp. Stop
ACME OFFICE BUILDING													
Cincinnati, Ohio													
RENT ROLL	Core Factor: R/U Ratio =		8.8%										
November 30, 2011													
100	Tenant 100	7,042		NNN	6		03/31/13					4.5%	
120	VACANT		2,707									1.7%	
150	VACANT		6,020									3.9%	
160	Tenant 160	1,822		NNN	4		03/31/15					1.2%	
180	VACANT		1,503									1.0%	
190	Tenant 190	1,103		NNN	3		07/31/14					0.7%	
200	Tenant 200	4,832		NNN	2		10/31/13					3.1%	
210	Tenant 210	4,161		NNN	7		11/30/14					2.7%	
230	Tenant 230	5,767					12/31/13					3.7%	
250	VACANT		5,130									3.3%	
290	VACANT		2,090									1.3%	
300	Tenant 300	2,844					09/30/14					1.8%	
375	Tenant 375	19,764					04/30/15					12.7%	
400	VACANT		8,933									5.8%	
430	VACANT		4,458									2.9%	
436	Tenant 436	1,557					01/31/14					1.0%	
440	Tenant 440	681					06/30/14					0.4%	
460	Tenant 460	4,786					01/31/14					3.1%	
490	VACANT		2,150									1.4%	
500	Tenant 500	22,570					03/31/14					14.6%	
600	VACANT		2,857									1.8%	
620	VACANT		1,143									0.7%	
630	Tenant 630	2,105					04/30/15					1.4%	
640	VACANT		2,961									1.9%	
650	Tenant 650	9,296					06/30/16					6.0%	
690	Tenant 690	4,208					09/30/16					2.7%	
700	Tenant 700	22,535					06/30/17					14.5%	

FIGURE 4-4: SAMPLE RENT ROLL (CONT.)

TOTALS		115,073	39,952					0.00	0.00		100.0%	
	TOTAL PROJECT SIZE	155,025										
	OCCUPANCY / VACANCY	74.2%	25.8%									

TENANT MIX AND PLACEMENT

When leasing an office building, a manager must give some consideration to the combination of selected tenants. The right *tenant mix* (the types of businesses that are carried out in the building and the stature of the individual tenants) will reinforce your building's position in the market and will locate the tenants in the way that best suits their needs.

Another reason to consider tenant mix is that tenants will naturally be interested in knowing with whom they share the address and what types of clients those other tenants will be attracting into the building. In order to provide the best tenant mix, consider the following factors:

- Type of space and its size and location
- Good fit for ground-floor tenants
- Best demographics to suit target market and property image

Classifying Tenants

Within an office building, numerous types of tenants can lease office space:

- Professional
- General office (sole proprietor or service provider)
- Retail
- Government
- Medical
- Nonprofit
- Data Centers
- Schools

Tenants are often categorized by:

- The product or service they provide (most common)
- The size of their space
- Operational requirements
- Image

A list of common tenant categories includes:

- Major Institutional/Professional
  - Banks

- Insurance companies
- Professionals
- Corporate headquarters
- General Commercial
  - Retail—parking is important, tenants are sales oriented
  - Smaller buildings, accessible to workers and markets
- Medical and/or Dental
  - Generally located near hospitals

Creating the Ideal Tenant Mix

Attracting the right tenant mix and allocating leasing space in the most efficient way can optimize building revenue. Compatibility among the selected tenants is an important guideline to creating an optimum tenant mix.

Finding the right group of tenants requires research. The types of tenants in the market area and in competing office buildings can have a powerful influence.

tips

The following checklist provides some factors to analyze:

CHECKLIST: ANALYZING TENANT MIX

☐ What is the dominant tenancy of the building?

☐ What are the successful types of tenants in the market area?

☐ What are the unsuccessful types of tenants in the market area?

☐ What works and doesn't work in other buildings?

☐ How and why are tenants in those buildings compatible?

☐ What role does the tenant play in creating or maintaining the image of the building?

☐ Is there a risk of having too many tenants in the same industry?

These questions should be considered when leasing the space initially and as spaces in the building become available for re-lease. It is important to establish a quality mix of tenants who pay rent in full and on time, willingly pay higher rent for desirable space, and contribute to the building's image.

When deciding upon the appropriate tenant mix for your building, consider the following factors:

- Professional versus general office
- Ground-floor tenants (amenity tenants)
- Controversial entities
- Financial stability

FACTOR	DESCRIPTION
Professional versus General Office 	• Some prospects actively avoid properties that also lease to a demographic with which they don't wish to associate • Example: executive-heavy corporations or professional firms may hesitate to lease space in a building whose tenancy includes a large presence of general office service providers (less prestige)
Ground-floor tenants (amenity tenants) 	• Ground-floor tenants should attract the most foot traffic from the general public and provide an amenity to other workers in the building • Examples: coffee shops, optical shops, candy stores, cellular stores, copy shops, banking, insurance, brokerage-type tenants, financial advisors • Ground-floor space in a building located in the CBD (especially retail core) typically commands the highest rents • Amenity tenants are attractive to tenants' employees and increase foot traffic from surrounding buildings • Example: drug store selling greeting cards and cosmetics as well as prescription and over-the-counter drugs • Consider existing tenants and neighborhood when identifying potential amenity tenants
Controversial Entities 	• Some government, social, or political organizations might be targets of protests and controversy causing civil disorder or damage to the property/people • Other examples: health care office disposing of medical waste, laboratories that use volatile chemicals
Financial Stability 	• Verifying financial stability for any tenant is crucial to ensure that the lease obligations can be met • Strive to establish a quality mix of tenants who pay rent in a timely manner and can contribute to the building's image

Tenant Placement

In addition to tenant mix, the location of tenants in an office building can impact the building's image. Examples:

- The top floor of a mid or high rise building in a Central Business District is a good location for quality restaurants
- Health clubs and printing facilities are good uses for basement (lower-level) space
- Ground-floor retail uses should represent the quality of the building and the office tenants

Parking and access should be appropriate for the type of tenant. Drug stores, banks, and insurance agencies need to accommodate large numbers of customers and high turnover, while tenants such as doctors' offices have patients who park for long periods of time. Tenants whose customers need long-term parking should be separated from those with conflicting parking requirements.

Leasing Retail Space in Office Buildings

Retail tenants bring multiple benefits to the office building, in addition to the potential for additional income. In cities with dense pedestrian traffic, ground-floor retail may produce the highest rent per square foot of any space in the building. The potential that retailers offer is in the ability to bring in percentage rent above the base rent. In addition, retailers can be marketed as an amenity to the office tenant prospects. In some cases, a retailer with good brand recognition may be seen as lending prestige to the location.

Bringing successful retailers to your building requires keen target marketing and a good sense of how to complement the tenant mix in your building and the other retailers in the area to meet the needs and wants of customers. Consider the following questions:

- What is the profile of the workers in the area?
- Do tourists have a large presence in the location?
- Is a convention center nearby?

In order to make the right choice:

- Make sure the retail activity is complementary to the office building tenants
- Conduct a market survey of retailers in the immediate area
- Understand the differences between base rent leases and percentage rent provisions

Resources:

More information on the retail component of commercial leasing is available in *Shopping Center Management and Leasing,* Richard F. Muhlebach and Alan A. Alexander, Institute of Real Estate Management, (2005).

Leasing Medical Office Buildings (MOBs)

The healthcare industry and healthcare real estate have changed dramatically in the past several years. Healthcare reform, the recession, lower reimbursements and other issues continue to drive changes. Almost every aspect of these properties is unique, so a brief overview of key information is presented in the following table.

MOB INFORMATION	DESCRIPTION
Ownership	• On campus MOBs may be owned by the hospital or by an owner/developer or REIT. The later almost always involve a ground lease. Management may be assigned to a hospital facilities group or to a third party leasing/management team. • Off campus MOBs may be owned by hospitals, medical practitioners occupying the building or investors including medical office REITS. Specialty buildings may be self-managed but when many assets are involved; medical providers may consolidate lease administration to a third party manager.
Leasing Issues	• Less opportunity for frequent renewals and re-leasing as medical tenants do not relocate as often as office tenants • Must manage costs effectively as most leases are NNN and buildings compete on operating expenses and tenant improvement dollars being offered as well as lease term • Hospitals control effective use restrictions in buildings on their campus and the leasing team must work with the hospital to gain approval of tenants. Increasingly, hospitals employ physicians on a direct basis so the leasing team negotiates with the hospital and not the physician for lease space in the building. If the hospital owns space, the leasing team must be aware of Stark laws and manage lease pricing accordingly. • Fewer buildings to lease, fewer prospects, and small space (less than 10,000 sq ft) may mean that brokers have little incentive, as the small market and commissions do not compete with larger office building leases

MOB
INFORMATION   DESCRIPTION

Tenant Profile
- On campus MOB rents are generally greater and profile may include more medical specialists and physicians directly affiliated with the hospital, large group practices, medical corporations, pharmacies, and non-medical uses.   Increasingly, higher acuity care uses such as surgery centers, radiation vaults, imaging centers, etc. have moved to MOBs to save costs.
- MOBs located in neighborhoods may be smaller, have lower rents, and are generally occupied by primary care physicians, dentists, and non-physician tenants
- In response to the new healthcare laws, many hospitals are building small surgical centers and freestanding emergency departments in areas away from larger hospitals

Attracting Tenants
- Develop relationships with hospital administration including physician relations team and keep them informed of space available in the property. Ground lease language for on campus buildings typically restricts landlord from leasing to tenants without hospital approval.
- Advertise in medical journals such as the American Medical Association journal. Attend medical conventions and trade shows. Maintain an active website listing vacant space.
- Develop strategic partnerships with large hospital systems representing the system in multiple transactions

Maintenance and Facility Management
- MOB tenants tend to have high service expectations. Additionally, standards and regulations in effect at the hospital carry over to the MOB when hospital services are relocated to the MOB. Must be aware of JAYCO standards related to all building systems and management team must be more sophisticated in its approach to documentation of required maintenance.
- Janitorial standards are higher due to use and type of facility and may range from general office cleaning for administrative areas to terminal clean in surgical centers or transplant areas. Cost for janitorial is greater than general office and strict standards must be followed in cleaning and medical waste removal.
- Experienced medical office space planners will address ADA compliance and understand the additional requirements for engineering and health standards associated with planning and building many of today's specialty medical spaces such as surgery centers

LEASING TO SIMILAR TENANTS	
PROS	CONS
• Synergy • Rent premiums • Attention and resources focused on known marketing efforts • Building can develop a reputation for a specific use	• Risk if the economy affects specific industries due to lack of diversification (potential for the entire building to become vacant) • Limits opportunity to maximize marketing reach • May create competition that affects everyone's bottom line

"Tenant mix and placement is all about being intentional. You always want to ask yourself, 'Did I mean to do this, or not?' Remember that you are working towards a tenant mix and placement strategy that optimizes success for both the owner and the other tenants."
–Stephen Cary, CPM®, Omaha, Nebraska

SPACE PLANNING

Space planning is an important component in the leasing process. It is particularly important during the early leasing stages. The real estate manager's role during this process is to:

- Consult with the tenant to determine needed space
- Ensure a balanced relationship between space and work flow
- Respond to the tenant's present space requirements
- Anticipate the tenant's future needs

Space planning meetings are conducted with the prospective tenant and the broker very early in the leasing process. The purpose of these meetings is to identify the specific square footage needs of the tenant and any special space requirements. It is important to show the prospect on paper where the office space will be situated and how the people and furniture will fit into the space.

Space planning is a major consideration when negotiating a lease because the cost of tenant improvements can have a tremendous impact on the economics of the deal. Consider the following best practices:

- Design the lease in accordance with the owner's objectives
- Assess net effective rent of various options—rent, term, and TI contributions

- Include any pertinent documentation related to space planning:
  - Special space requirements
  - Above-standard tenant improvements
  - Floor load requirements
  - Adjacencies of work flow

An increasingly social, mobile, and collaborative work style continues to impact space planning and design configuration trends. Tenants may be asking for reduced square footage as well as design considerations that maximize flexibility and collaboration. Real estate managers must partner with their tenants in order to meet evolving space requirement and reconfiguration needs.

The Benefits of Space Planning Management

It is important to take an active approach to space planning discussions. Effective space planning offers the following benefits:

- Protects the owner's interest.
- Maintains the value of the property.
- Optimizes leasable space for the tenant while maximizing the dollar return. The greater your space efficiency, the more likely you are to close the deal.
- Enhances the property and its position in the market.

FIGURE 4-5: SAMPLE SPACE PLAN

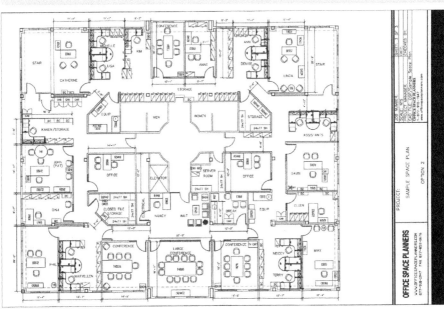

Source: Office Space Planners (www.officespaceplanners.com).

Professional Space Planners

Although property managers generally oversee the space planning process, most leasing companies employ professional space planners, either in-house or job-by-job. An experienced space planner can use certain basic information about the prospective tenants (e.g., for a law firm, the number of partners, associates, clerks, administrative support, and conference rooms) to design a reasonably efficient and representative office in a first draft. For management companies who do not have in-house expertise, a variety of professional space planners are available to draw upon.

FACTOR	DESCRIPTION
Interior Design Firms	• Are allies in leasing space
	• Should provide design in accordance with building standards and tenant's image and budget, and involve the least amount of space possible
	• Should deal with the prospect only in your presence—may try to sell additional services and furniture
Major Architectural Firms	• May provide free or discounted services in exchange for the opportunity to complete construction drawing
	• Can be complex in terms of working through building codes, standard building material, and rounds of edits
Office Furniture Companies	• Often offer their services free or at a discount depending on the size of furniture purchase
Space Planning Firm	• Can be used to show prospect how the existing space can be adapted
	• Is particularly useful in soft markets
	• Tenants may use their services at their expense to suit their needs
	• Services provided are usually preliminary drawings and final construction drawings (CDs) including floor plans, electrical, mechanical, reflective ceiling plan, and finish specification

**Stephen Cary, CPM®
Omaha, Nebraska**

Case Study: Space Planning

Space planning discussions can be a great way to engage the prospective client and get them excited about the space. I sometimes have the space planner make a small error on the first draft of a space plan to get a reaction from the tenant such as, "This looks good, but we talked about the kitchen over here." The result is that the tenants are beginning to imagine themselves in the space. They're invested and excited to move forward with the leasing process.

Speed to market and quick decisions are critical components of space planning. Deals are often lost because the space isn't ready. Today's tenants are sophisticated and technologically savvy. They have plenty of resources and information and come prepared with space planning knowledge.

tips

Space Planning: Guidelines for Space Allocation

1. DETERMINE A PROSPECT'S NEEDS

The prospect's needs should be tracked and recorded, including:

- Kind of work that is done at the firm
- Firm's desired image
- Number of staff and plans for expanding the staff
- Organizational chart—What does it look like and how does the company's organization and culture affect the use of space?
- Budget guidelines

CHECKLIST: TENANT SPACE NEEDS

- ☐ Space for executives in relation to the support staff (placement)
- ☐ Private office versus open space (privacy needs and corporate culture)
- ☐ Offices with windows or natural light
- ☐ Desired reception area
- ☐ Accessibility and visibility of offices from reception area
- ☐ Visitor traffic, location of meeting areas, special A/V needs
- ☐ Size and type of furniture and work stations and office equipment
- ☐ Finish level required (non-standard or standard)
- ☐ Personnel traffic and access (e.g., location of confidential files)
- ☐ Lighting, ceilings, HVAC, electrical, telecommunications
- ☐ Expansion space desired
- ☐ Fire and safety regulations
- ☐ Special requirements (e.g., vaults, storerooms, library, copying)

When making space planning changes to the building, keep in mind that tenant modifications may impact the building core. It is important to keep data on how these changes have affected the floor load in order to safeguard against possible structural ramifications for the building core.

2. CONSIDER GENERAL LAYOUT PRINCIPLES

A space planner must keep certain general principles in mind in preparing a layout:

CHECKLIST: GENERAL LAYOUT PRINCIPLES

☐ All work stations, whether in a private office or open area, should be reduced to units of furniture and equipment

☐ Electrical and computer needs may limit planning considerations if access is a problem—particularly in older buildings

☐ Employees should be provided with lighting suited to their work

☐ Storage needs should be assessed (e.g., access to storage on-site, hanging space for coats, and shelves for hats and packages)

☐ Heavy equipment should generally be placed against walls or columns to avoid overloading. Know floor-load capabilities

☐ Layout must comply with fire safety codes governing aisles, exits, stairwells, and other parts of the structure

3. USE A CHECKLIST FOR THE PRELIMINARY PLAN

A preliminary plan and drawings must include certain factors:

CHECKLIST: PRELIMINARY PLAN

☐ Know what furniture and equipment will fit into the space

☐ Make sure that department and room layouts can be seen clearly

☐ Show space in relation to building common areas such as elevators and restrooms

☐ Show room dimensions clearly

☐ Provide a legend of the scale and symbols used

☐ Show door openings and windows

FIGURE 4-6: TENANT SPACE REQUIREMENT QUESTIONNAIRE

Building _____ Floor/Suite/Exposure _____

Tenant Name _____ Length of Lease Term _____

Contact/Title _____ Phone _____

Present Address _____

Reason for Move _____

Present/Future Employees _____/_____ in Offices _____/_____ in Cubicles _____/_____ in Open Area

General Space Needs		Est. Sq Ft
Mail Room	No. and Type of Machines	
	Freight Access Needed ☐ Yes ☐ No	
	Floor Site Important ☐ Yes ☐ No	
	Traffic ☐ Heavy ☐ Medium ☐ Light	
	Comments	
Copy Center(s)	☐ Yes ☐ Alcove ☐ No. and Type of Machines	
	Location	
Computer Room	☐ Yes ☐ No Special Needs	
Library	☐ Yes ☐ No Special Needs	
Lunchroom/Lounge	☐ Yes ☐ No Special Needs	
Conference Room	☐ Yes ☐ No How Many No. of People	
	Table Size/Shape Special Needs	
Central Files	☐ Separate ☐ Not Separate Special Needs	
Vault	☐ Yes ☐ No Special Needs	
Closets	How Many Size Each Special Needs	
Additional Storage	☐ Yes ☐ No Special Needs_____	
	In Basement ☐ Yes ☐ No Comments	
Reception Area	Switchboard ☐ Yes ☐ No Furniture	
	No. Visitors/Day Special Needs	
Parking	No. of Spaces	
	Subtotal of Estimated Square Feet	
Equipment		
Communications	No. of Telephones No. of Incoming Lines Intercom ☐ Yes ☐ No	
Office Machines	Personal Computers Electric Typewriters Photocopiers _____	
	Computer Printers Other Peripherals (No./Type)	
Special Needs for Equipment	Water 125 Watts Electricity	
	Special Soundproofing Special HVAC Auxiliary Power	

FIGURE 4-6: TENANT SPACE REQUIREMENT QUESTIONNAIRE *(CONT)*

Name/Title	Old Office Size	New Office Size	Contents	Special Requirements	Est. Sq Ft

No. of Offices	Private	Semi-Private	Subtotal	
			Subtotal from Previous Page	
			+ 15% for Traffic Flow	
			Total Square Feet	

NOTE: These sample forms and agreements are not endorsed by the Institute of Real Estate Management. They are presented for informational purposes only and should not be relied upon for accuracy, completeness, or consistency with applicable law. The user is advised to check all applicable state and federal law before using these forms, agreements, or parts thereof. Because certain forms have legal implications (e.g., management agreements, rental applications), it is recommended that downloaded versions of such forms should be reviewed with legal counsel prior to their use and that any modifications made by the user should also be reviewed by legal counsel.

Resources:

Forms such as a floor data card, tenant space requirements questionnaire, tenant construction cost estimates, and space planning services schedule can be found on www. irem.org.

TI Construction: Economics of the Lease

Once space needs have been determined, it is necessary to plan for construction. Estimating the cost of tenant improvement (TI) work is extremely important in order to understand the economics of the lease transaction. This estimate becomes the Year 0 input for a Discounted Cash Flow analysis of the lease transaction in order to achieve a desired effective rent. Factors that should be considered include:

- **PROPERTY TAX IMPLICATIONS:** Should tax increases resulting from substantial TI work be attributable to a single tenant? Are tracking and calculation mechanisms in place to assess the dollar amount of the increase?

- **CODE COMPLIANCE ISSUES TRIGGERED BY TI WORK:** Is the building grandfathered? Does the specific TI require adherence to codes not required for building? Is this code compliance a tenant expense or a building expense?

Once the costs are identified, the manager must consider several lease options:

- **TURNKEY:** Landlord will perform specified improvements at its sole cost

- **TI ALLOWANCE:** The tenant will be provided a fixed dollar amount or specified dollar per usable square foot of leased space to complete improvements

- **AS-IS:** Landlord is providing the space in its current condition and has no obligation or responsibility for improvements during the term of the lease

- **AMORTIZED TI:** The landlord will provide TI cost up front but will add that cost to the tenant's monthly rent over the term of the lease. CAUTION: A tenant with good credit and financial knowledge can typically borrow TI dollars at a lower cost on the open market. A tenant unable to obtain funds from alternate sources may have financial constraints the landlord should be aware of in underwriting the lease.

- **MIDTERM IMPROVEMENTS:** The landlord can commit to providing improvements at a specified point during the lease term. This is an effective tool if the landlord does not have the funds, if the tenant is a credit risk, or if the improvements are not essential today but will be during the term of the lease.

Construction Planning

Planning for TI work is no different than planning for general construction projects. Be sure to examine the following issues related to financing and insurance:

- Funds available from capital budgeting for replacement
- Availability of loans and loan application procedures
- Collateral available for a loan (e.g., leases can be used as collateral for a loan because they are contracts)
- Funds available from capital budgeting for replacement
- Lenders' insurance requirements
- Insurance needs for construction (e.g., workers' compensation)
- Contractors' insurance (e.g., the contractors' liability coverage and workers' compensation)
- Scheduling

Planning a tenant improvement project involves a fairly long schedule and a number of participants. The first few steps involve testing whether the proposal is viable. You should sketch out suitable alternatives to test as well—such as a longer lease term, higher rental rate, and/or lower tenant improvement allowance. The key word is *compare*—compare alternatives, costs, bids, prices, and schedules.

FIGURE 4-7: COST/BENEFIT ANALYSIS

- ☐ **FORMULATE A PLAN OF ACTION FOR EACH ALTERNATIVE.** Outline what needs to be done in each case (factor in costs such as materials and labor; outside contractors; professional services by architects, lawyers, accountants, and engineers; overtime pay for staff; rent loss due to construction; financing costs; permits; and other fees and commissions). If costs outweigh benefits to the property's value, the proposed project is not economically feasible. Eliminate unworkable alternatives early in the process.

- ☐ **IDENTIFY THE CONTRACTORS AND VENDORS NEEDED.** Test alternatives financially by asking for preliminary estimates from suppliers.

- ☐ **ESTIMATE THE FINANCIAL FEASIBILITY OF EACH ALTERNATIVE.** Return on investment should increase as a result of the construction.

- ☐ **CONSULT WITH THE OWNERS REGARDING THEIR WISHES TO PURSUE THE RENOVATION.** Offer all the information you have gathered. If the decision is favorable, you can move into a planning phase and begin to carry out the alternative that was agreed upon.

- ☐ **APPLY FOR FINANCING, AS NEEDED, AND PLAN FOR INSURANCE NEEDS.**

- ☐ **INFORM CONTRACTORS AND SUPPLIERS AND BEGIN TO FIRM UP ESTIMATES, PLANS, AND SCHEDULES** (preliminary and working drawings).

- ☐ **PREPARE A PLAN TO EXECUTE WORK.** Include schedule and flow of work and who will do the work (e.g., employees or contractors).

- ☐ **REMEMBER TO CONSIDER THE IMPACT OF THE WORK ON CURRENT TENANTS** (if the building will be occupied during construction).

- ☐ **DETERMINE WHETHER RENOVATION WILL HAVE A WIDER IMPACT.** Plans to alter or demolish a historic building have caused controversies in many cities.

- ☐ **REMEMBER TO GET ALL NECESSARY PERMITS.** If the permits are not in order, the city or other local regulatory agency can stop work. Special permits may be required (e.g., building in a historic district).

After comparing alternatives, the next phase is characterized by planning and organizing. Preliminary drawings, working drawings, draft schedules, and work assignments may all change before work actually begins.

The final phase is to ensure that the construction is completed with minimal disruption to the regular operations of the property. The real estate manager should focus on three courses of action to monitor the progress and quality of work:

- Supervise the progress actively
- Make sure the work stays on schedule
- Meet with contractors and other parties to make sure they are monitoring progress and can complete the work on schedule

Construction management is a growing profit center for management companies that expand the space planning process to include construction bidding, contracting, and value-added tenant improvements. Being able to supervise construction that is taking place on the property is an added benefit.

tips

QUALIFYING PROSPECTS

Once a serious prospect is identified, it is necessary to assess the prospect's overall desirability as a tenant for the building. This process is called *qualifying*. Only the most highly qualified prospects should be considered for tenancy. The following table shows important factors to consider in prospect qualification.

FACTOR	CONSIDERATIONS
Space Requirements	• Can your property accommodate the specific space requirements of the prospect?
	• Determine if prospect seriously wants to move or expand facilities by determining when their current lease expires.
	• Consider the density of the occupant and the impact on parking.
Financial Strength and Stability	• Perhaps most important area to assess.
	• Does the tenant prospect have the ability and willingness to contribute to their tenant improvement costs?
	• **BUSINESS HISTORY:** Consider number of years in business, but financial success is more important. Request business plan for new companies.
	• **PERSONAL GUARANTEES:** Investigate how the business is constituted as a legal entity, request articles of incorporation if prospect claims to be corporation, ensure lease signer is authorized in company.

FACTOR	CONSIDERATIONS
Financial Strength and Stability *(Continued)*	• **FINANCIAL STATEMENTS:** Prospects should submit financial statement outlining income and expenses, loan obligations, and other outstanding debt (confidential). Ask for pro forma projections for at least three years. Financial statement should match entity on the lease to reflect true ability to pay rent. A balance sheet provides financial position at a point in time. Assess working capital, current ratio, and net worth to measure liquidity (refer to Figure 4-8). • **CREDIT RATING:** Get two credit references if small business/first-time tenant in addition to references from landlord, call suppliers or utility companies, use Dun & Bradstreet, Standard & Poor's, and Experian Business Reports for large- and medium-sized companies (web-enabled).
Service Requirements	• Consider security, HVAC, business hours, and other service. • Analyze the actual costs and cost/benefit ratio over the long term. May be worth the effort if prospect is more willing to seek long-term lease, and if effort attracts other similar prospects.
Qualifying Retail Prospects	• Evaluate financial strength and stability; business history and operations; reputation, promotion, and merchandise presentation; customer service, store hours, annual sales, and sales per square foot in their other stores (if applicable). • Ask for pro forma projections of sales reports or projections for at least three years.

FIGURE 4-8: WORKING CAPITAL, CURRENT RATIO, AND NET WORTH FORMULAS

Working capital is the difference between total current assets and total current liabilities (anything that will convert to cash within the next 12 months).

Working Capital = Current Assets – Current Liabilities

The *current ratio* shows the ability to pay current bills with funds on hand and indicates the company's liquidity. ("Current" indicates transactions that occur in the short term (90 days). "Total" indicates long-term transactions). Be certain to evaluate these in light of the new lease at your property.

Current Ratio = Current Assets ÷ Current Liabilities

Net worth is the total assets less total liabilities.

Net Worth = Total Assets – Total Liabilities

FIGURE 4-9: SAMPLE BALANCE SHEET

Burton Place Building, INC.
Balance Sheet
December 31, 2---

ASSETS	
Current Assets	
Cash	1,052
Accounts Receivable	63,417
Tenant Deposits	101,600
Tax Escrow	110,000
Prepaid Insurance	10,000
Capital Reserves	15,000
Total Current Assets	301,069
Long-Term Assets	
Land	500,000
Buildings	2,000,000
Less Depreciation	(72,800)
Net Buildings	1,927,200
Total Assets	2,728,269
LIABILITIES	
Current Liabilities	
Tenant Direct Payable	101,600
Accounts Payable	12,500
Tax Payable	120,000
Total Current Liabilities	234,100
Long-Term Liabilities	
Mortgage Payable	2,294,202
Total Liabilities	2,528,302
Net Worth (Owner's Equity)	199,967
Total Liabilities and Equity	2,728,269

For more information on how to determine an acceptable ratio of assets to liabilities, refer to the IREM course "Investment Real Estate: Financial Tools (FIN402)."

CHAPTER 4:
Resources

Publications:

Muhlebach, Richard F., and Alexander, Alan A., *Shopping Center Management and Leasing*. Chicago: Institute of Real Estate Management, 2005.

Websites:

www.irem.org/resources/by-topic/leasing (IREM Resources: Leasing)

Formulating the Lease

This book follows the typical timeline of an office building lease deal. The timeline below shows where we are within the process.

Understanding Office Buildings	Assessing the Market	Developing Marketing Plans	Developing Leasing Plans	**Formulating the Lease**	Retaining Tenants

Analyzing, comparing, and negotiating lease terms can maximize the financial outcome for the owner. A property manager must be able to understand major lease provisions and clauses and their impact on the property's financial health.

What's in this chapter:

- The Lease Document
- Lease Negotiation
- Lease Analysis

THE LEASE DOCUMENT

The *lease* can be defined as a written contract for the conveyance of occupancy rights for part or all of an owner or landlord's property for a stipulated period of time in consideration of the payment of rent or other compensation by the tenant. The lease is a legally binding contract that outlines each party's obligations and responsibilities to the other party. Its terms should reflect the needs and desires, and protect the interests, of both parties.

No uniform lease document could cover every possible agreement between a tenant and an owner. However, many organizations have a standard lease form that provides a basis for subsequent lease negotiations. Legal counsel should be sought with regard to developing a standard lease form and making any negotiated changes to the lease.

Basic Elements

The lease document will always include standard basic elements:

CHECKLIST: BASIC LEASE ELEMENTS

- ☐ Identification and signatures of parties to the lease
- ☐ Description of the leased premises
- ☐ Term (duration) of the lease
- ☐ Statement of intended use of the premises by the tenant
- ☐ Rent and other charges
- ☐ Provisions of the office lease
- ☐ Rules and regulations

IDENTIFICATION OF PARTIES

A lease begins by identifying the owner or landlord, the tenant, and any other parties involved, such as a broker or *guarantor* (one who assumes responsibility for a financial obligation of another in the event the other person cannot perform). It is important to indicate whether the parties are sole proprietorships, corporations, or partnerships and to describe their relationship to each other through the lease agreement and their specific authority to sign it.

PARTIES	DESCRIPTION
Sole Proprietorship 	• One-person business • One individual personally responsible for paying rents and meeting other financial obligations
Partnerships 	• Slightly more complicated • Partners identified individually on the first page of the lease and sign their names on the last or signature page • Nature of the partnership should be stated, as this has bearing on the liability of each partner
General Partnership 	• Debts and liabilities shared by all of the general partners
Limited Partnership 	• Each limited partner is usually financially liable only up to the value of his or her proportionate investment • Usually one or more general partners who carry full liability
Corporation 	• Entity that is liable for obligations under a contract, although some personal liability may accrue to its officers or board of directors under certain circumstances. • Sometimes when a corporation is a tenant it may be necessary to secure a personal guaranty of the financial obligations under the lease.

PARTIES	DESCRIPTION
Corporation (Cont.)	• Can be complicated entities (e.g., parent company, wholly owned subsidiary, holding company). Due diligence should be used to determine the most viable entity for the lease.
Limited Liability Corporation (LLC) 	• Business structure with corporation and partnership qualities • Provides protection from individual liabilities like corporations and tax advantages of a partnership • Some states also acknowledge the limited liability partnership, which protects individual partners from liability of employees under their control

DESCRIPTION OF LEASED PREMISES

To describe the premises, the lease should include the following:

- Correct street address
- Location of leased space in building
- Method of measuring leased space (rentable and usable area) and size of the space
- Identification of the building's total square footage acknowledging the tenant's proportionate share
- Site plans or floor plans displaying location and configuration

LEASE TERM

The following items should be stated as part of the lease term:

- Duration of the lease (term start and end dates)
- Date of execution
- Date of tenant occupancy (move-in)
- Commencement date of rental payments

USE OF PREMISES

Use of premises refers to the type of business that the tenant can conduct in the space; this is one of the most important clauses in the lease. Tenants typically want to negotiate a broad use clause, such as "general office use," while landlords typically want a more narrow definition. The use clause will affect what a tenant may do in the space in the future, and it will affect any sublease and/or assignment rights the tenant may have. This intended use must be legal, and any other use, such as residential occupancy, should be strictly prohibited.

Avoid potentially harmful, unclear descriptions in the Use of Premises clause, such as, "general business."

RENT AND OTHER CHARGES

The lease document should clearly state:

- Amount of base and/or percentage rent
- When the rent is due, when the rent is delinquent, and where the rent is to be paid
- Amount of the security deposit (if any)
- First month's rent if it will be different
- Date rent payment commences

Rental rates and other charges vary for each space and should be in line with the owner's goals and objectives for the property.

Commercial Rents

Rents are commonly stated in office leases in one of three ways:

- Base rent
- Percentage rent
- Combination of the two

When establishing rent structure, it is extremely important to consider the financial impact of *operating expense recovery,* an integral part of determining net effective rent and capturing the value of the lease. Two common methods of billing the tenants for their shares of the building's operating expenses are:

- **BASE YEAR APPROACH.** The owner establishes the initial rent using existing levels of taxes, insurance, and maintenance. These costs are then built into the lease rental rate, and during the term of the lease, the owner pays the expenses up to the amount established in the base year.
- **EXPENSE STOP APPROACH.** The costs for operating the building at a certain occupancy percentage are calculated and broken down to a square footage basis. This figure is then built into the rents; the owner is responsible for the established amount, and the tenants pay any increases above that level for each year of the lease.

BASE RENT

Base rent is the rent per rentable or usable square foot per year, usually paid in regular monthly installments. It can be based on market rents, which are determined by comparing rents of similar properties.

Base rental rates vary from one region to another and may also be affected by the age and location of the building. A new property may have larger financial commitments to meet, and thus may charge higher rents. On the other hand, an existing building may sustain higher rents than a new building can command because it has already been successfully established.

Base rent is always part of a standard office lease because it offers advantages for both the owner and the tenant:

- **OWNER:** Assures a fixed level of income
- **TENANT:** Guarantees a set amount of rent to be paid for the duration of the lease (budgeted for specifically)

PERCENTAGE RENT

Percentage rent applies to retail tenants leasing a space. For retailers, percentage rent involves the tenant paying the owner a percentage of gross sales in addition to the base rent, or the greater of the two.

If a tenant's sales volume does not reach the sales break point, no percentage rent will be required and the tenant will pay the minimum base rent. Retail rents are always higher per square foot than office space rents in the same building. Gross sales should be reported by the tenant and should be audited if necessary. Keep in mind that a dollar of percentage rent is not equal to a dollar of base rent to the owner since percentage rent is not guaranteed.

There are several ways to compute percentage rent. One method involves paying percentage rent with a guaranteed base rent. For example, the lease might state that the tenant will pay five percent of gross sales with a minimum annual rent of $60,000. This scenario will usually require payment to be made in equal monthly installments.

Breakpoints

The amount of gross sales at which the percentage rent equals the minimum rent is referred to as the *natural breakpoint.*

Some leases may be negotiated to include an *artificial breakpoint,* a dollar amount of gross sales that is higher or lower than the natural breakpoint. An artificial breakpoint may be negotiated in cases in which the landlord has to make more extensive improvements to a shell space than the typical tenant improvement allowance would cover. In such cases, the owner may agree to the larger tenant improvement expense and lower the breakpoint so the retailer will begin paying percentage rent on a smaller sales volume sooner. In this way, the owner is gradually repaid for the cost of the improvements without changing the base rent. However, note that retail tenants are typically used to and expect to pay for their tenant improvements. Landlords typically deliver shell space only.

ESCALATION OF RENTS

Most owners cannot accurately predict what their expenses will be in the future due to changes in the market and the economy. Inflation alone would debilitate a building if there were no protections for the owner who holds a long-term gross lease calling for fixed minimum rates. Thus, most long-term leases include an *escalation clause* calling for regular increases in the base rent.

The escalation clause permits the rent to be adjusted to accommodate changes due to inflation and may be based on the Consumer Price Index (CPI), in which the cost of goods is compared across the country.

The rent increase is computed by dividing the CPI for the current year by the CPI for the previous year. This ratio is then multiplied by the current monthly rent to yield the new rental rate.

(CPI Current Year ÷ CPI Previous Year) × Current Monthly Rent = New Monthly Rent

Example:

If the CPI for the current year is 184.2 and the CPI for last year was 178.8, then the ratio of the CPI for the two years is as follows:

184.2 ÷ 178.8 = 1.03

This figure is then multiplied by the current rent to determine the new rent:

1.03 × $1,000 = $1,030 New Rent

Other methods of increasing rents include specific incremental increases stated in the lease as specific amounts or specific percentages. The lease should clearly define the method of calculating rent escalations and when they are to occur (yearly, every other year, and so forth) as well as what is meant by "base year," "price index," "lease year," and any other terms to be used in the computations. When using an index such as the Consumer Price Index, be sure to select a month sufficiently prior to the lease commencement date that the data will be published and available.

FIGURE 5-1: SAMPLE CPI LEASE LANGUAGE

SAMPLE 1

Beginning with the second year of the lease and annually thereafter, the lease payment will be increased by the percentage increase of the Consumer Price Index from the previous year's increase.

SAMPLE 2

(a) The term "Price Index" shall mean the "Consumer Price Index" published by the Bureau of labor statistics of the United States Department of Labor, All Items, New York, NY—Northeastern, NJ for urban consumers.
(b) The term "Base Price Index" shall mean the Price Index for the year prior to the attained year commencing upon the 2nd anniversary of the lease term.
(c) The term "Current Price Index" shall mean the Price Index for the first month of each lease year's anniversary.

If the Current Price Index for any lease year shall be greater than the Base Price Index, the base rent shall be increased by an amount equal to product obtained by multiplying

(i) the percentage difference between the Current Price Index and the Base Price Index by
(ii) the fixed rent (such increase hereinafter referred to as the "Cost of Living Adjustment").

However, in no event shall Owner have any obligation to Tenant hereunder if the Current Price Index for any lease year is less than the Base Price Index, or

1. In no event shall an annual escalation exceed 50% of the CPI increase as aforementioned computed or:
2. In no event shall an annual escalation as aforementioned computed be less than 1% or greater than 4%.

Source: Maltz, John, "CPI Escalations: The Evolution of an Index," Real Estate Weekly, June 2, 2004.

OPERATING EXPENSES

Whether a lease calls for payment of base rent, percentage rent, or both, tenants may also pay a portion of the overall costs of operating the property. Keep the following considerations in mind:

- Typically, expenses for the coming year are estimated and each tenant is presented a list of prorated charges
- One-twelfth of this share is due at the beginning of each month
- At the end of the year, the owner prepares an annual statement showing actual expenses compared to the estimate and the amount the tenant paid for expenses during the year
- Overpayments are typically credited toward the next year's expense proration
- If the settlement statement shows that the tenant owes money to the owner, this amount will be due within a certain time period, usually 30 days

The leasing agent's challenge in regard to determining operating expenses for tenants' rent, is deciding what constitutes "actual expenses." *Grossing-up* is the process of estimating what the operating expenses of a property would be if it were fully leased. The actual operating expenses for a building that is not completely full are either fixed or variable. To "gross-up" this figure is to project the actual operating expenses of the property to the level of being fully leased.

Grossing-up is a sound financial practice of real estate management because it provides a stable foundation for making financial comparisons during the lease term. When applied to the structure of an individual lease, it offers the following advantages:

- **OWNER:** Protected from inflationary risks during the lease term
- **TENANT:** Protected from unpredictable operating expense adjustments

Example:

- The example office building is 100,000 square feet.
- A tenant occupies 10,000 square feet in that building.
- The tenant pays a 10 percent pro rata share of the operating expenses.
- Janitorial costs are $1 per square foot.
- The cost for janitorial services at 100 percent building occupancy would be $100,000.
- The cost for janitorial services for the 10,000-square-foot tenant would be $10,000 (10,000 square feet x $1 per square foot).
- The building is only 50 percent occupied.
- The cost for janitorial services for the half-occupied building is $50,000 (50,000 square feet x $1 per square foot).
- If the tenant is charged his pro rata share of 10 percent, the charge is only $5,000 ($50,000 x 0.10) for janitorial services, while the actual cost to clean the tenant's premises is $10,000.
- When operating expenses are grossed-up to 100 percent occupancy, the cost for janitorial services is stated at $100,000 (100,000 square feet x $1 per square foot) and the tenant is billed $10,000 (10,000 square feet x $1), which is the actual janitorial cost for the tenant's space regardless of the building's occupancy level.

Source: Alexander, Alan A. and Muhlebach, Richard F., Lease Administration Simplified: A Real Estate Manager's Guide to Fair & Effective Lease Administration. IREM, 2009.

If subleasing is prevalent in your market area, consider the following tips:

- Subtenants should be in a similar industry as the main tenant
- Subtenants may help give the impression of a highly occupied building
- Do not give subtenants the same rights as the main tenants

tips

Provisions of the Office Lease

In addition to the use of premises clause discussed earlier, office leases have countless other provisions. A successful office building conveys a sense of unity to the customer, and therefore, the lease will include many clauses to support this. The following are typical office lease clauses listed in alphabetical order:

CLAUSE	DESCRIPTION
After Hours HVAC	• Clause states up front the policy on who pays the cost for HVAC after a defined period of business hours. • Responsibility of the tenant as described in the terms of the provision.
Alterations	• Tenants are prohibited from changing or making improvements to their leased spaces without written approval of the owner. • Alterations might violate local building codes or lower the property value.
Assignment and Subletting	• Most leases limit the tenant's right to assign or sublease the premises without the landlord's written consent. • Leases typically prohibit tenant from profiting on any sublease transaction. • Owner may feel the subtenant is of lesser quality or financial worth. • Lease should state that, at the time of sublease or assignment, the original tenant must have fulfilled all of its obligations. • Clause should require tenant to serve as guarantor if the sublessee (or subtenant) defaults.

CLAUSE	DESCRIPTION
Assignment and Subletting (Cont.)	• Language should cover both up and down markets. • Manager should ensure subtenant's letter of credit is current. • Related to subleasing is the take back or recapture clause, in which the owner has the right to terminate the current tenant's lease, take back the space, and lease it to a new tenant, possibly at a higher rent. Legal counsel should be consulted about the release of an assignor if the lease is assigned and the clause clarified; in most cases, it is best not to release an assignor.
Cancellation Options	• Options always favor the tenant and should not be granted without the owner receiving something in return. Cancellation options, although rare, should be reciprocal. • Kickout and Escape clauses allow the tenant to cancel or terminate the lease under certain conditions

Condemnation, Damage, and Destruction	• A clause that states the agreed rights, privileges, and limitations of the owner and tenant in case:
	  – Property is taken over for public use
	  – Use of the property is terminated for nonconformance with governmental regulations or hazards to public health and safety
	  – Property is damaged or destroyed
	• Clause should state tenant's rights if the leased premises are damaged or destroyed, including procedures for handling repairs.
	• A destruction clause is intended to prevent a tenant from terminating the lease because of partial destruction of the premises. If damage is extensive, the owner may terminate the lease, rather than make repairs, and the tenant would not be liable.

Default	• This clause states exactly what constitutes default and outlines what is to be done if either party defaults (nonperformance of lease terms). • The owner may have certain rights, including the right to regain possession of the space when a tenant defaults. • Real estate managers should consult with their attorneys if they are considering enacting the default clause. • The owner may hold the defaulting tenant responsible for continued payment of rent.

CLAUSE	DESCRIPTION

Estoppel	• Estoppel certificates are generally required when the property is being refinanced or sold.
	
	• Estoppel assures the lender or potential purchaser that the owner is receiving nothing more for the property than the rent that is stated in the lease and that there are no outstanding claims on the property.
	
	• By signing an estoppel certificate, the tenant affirms the following:
	  – The status and terms of the lease
	  – The full amount of the rent to be paid for the entire term of the lease.
	  – When rent is paid
	  – If any rent has been prepaid
	
	• The clause may also include information regarding the condition of the premises; adjustments, supplements, and amendments of the terms of the lease, if any; the existence of any condition of default on the tenant's part; and whether the owner has completed the promised improvements and repairs.

Expense Stops	• These clauses set the level at which the tenant begins contributing to the building's operating expenses. • They are negotiable and can favor either the landlord or the tenant, depending on the market conditions of the area.
Guaranty of Lease	• This clause states that in case of tenant default, the rent will be paid and the tenant's other obligations under the lease will be performed by a third party. • If a prospective tenant does not meet credit and financial strength criteria, the landlord may require additional corporate (parent organization) or individual guaranties consistent with financial statements provided if the lease is in the name of a "shell" corporation, a newly formed corporation, or an individual (sole proprietor).
Hold Harmless	• The landlord will not be liable for any injuries or damages sustained in, on, or about the tenant's leased premises or building common areas as a result of negligence or deliberate acts of the tenant's employees or visitors.
Holdover	• The holdover provision sets the terms of tenancy if a tenant does not vacate at lease termination. • Tenancy then becomes month-to-month under the terms and conditions of the original lease, subject to an increase in the base rent for the period of holdover.

CLAUSE	DESCRIPTION
Holdover (Cont.)	• The scheduled increase in base rent should be designed to motivate a renewal of the lease (if desired by the landlord) or a move-out (to facilitate move-in of a tenant to whom the space has been re-leased).
Insurance	• Office building owners usually buy insurance on the building and standard improvements to it, including fire and extended coverage, as well as general liability insurance. • Building insurance is charged back to tenants as an operating expense; it does not cover the contents of the tenant's leased premises. • Tenants are also required to obtain premises liability insurance and to insure their contents.
Late Charges	• Landlord may assess a late fee if tenant does not pay the rent by a predetermined date. • A grace period and a requirement for written notice to the tenant before assessment of the fee may be included in the lease along with the amount (or percentage rate) to be paid. • Late charges should apply to additional rent, not just minimum fixed rent.
Maintenance of Tenant's Premises	• Tenant is responsible for all maintenance and repairs within the leased premises. • Landlord is to maintain exterior walls, roof, foundation, and structural portions of the building outside the tenant's demised premises (may be included in maintenance costs charged back to tenants). • In some markets, the landlord may retain responsibility for some or all maintenance inside tenants' premises. • Provision should detail which party is responsible for any maintenance, repairs, and replacements.
Quiet Enjoyment	• Tenant is given the right to occupy the space without disturbances from other tenants and unannounced intrusions by the landlord, provided the tenant complies fully with the lease terms.
Relocation	• This clause grants the landlord the right to relocate the tenant's premises within the building, to combine spaces to attract a large tenant, or to protect a location for future expansion of a valuable tenant. • Tenants may seek a right of first refusal to allow for their future flexibility.

CLAUSE	DESCRIPTION
Rules and Regulations	• Landlords usually set rules to address issues of conformity and safety for the benefit of all. • Typical constraints are loading/unloading, shipping and deliveries; accumulation of trash and general housekeeping; office temperature and other aspects of the office building environment; and employee parking.
Security Deposit	• Typically one month's rent, a security deposit is required as a guaranty of the tenant's faithful performance under the lease. • The deposit may be applied to late charges and other payments due the landlord or to pay for repairs that are the tenant's responsibility. • Large tenants with established credit ratings may be able to negotiate this provision out of their leases; a letter of credit in a set amount may be required in lieu of a security deposit.
Signage	• The owner should set limits on the type and number of signs that a tenant can display on the property in order to control the appearance of the building. • Signage criteria should be established, including the landlord's right of approval; compliance with local laws may be an added consideration.
Subordination, Non-Disturbance, and Attornment (SNDA)	• The "subordination" portion permits a lender-mortgagee of the property whose lien is junior or subordinated to the tenant's (usually because the lease was recorded before the lien of the mortgage), to become superior to the lien of the lease. • If the owner declares bankruptcy or transfers ownership of the property in a foreclosure, tenants will be understandably concerned about being evicted or having to completely renegotiate the terms of their leases, and they will want to be assured of their rights and status under these circumstance. A non-disturbance agreement permits the lease to stay in force as long as the tenant is not in default. • The attornment agreement creates a contractual bond between the tenant and a third-party mortgagee, pursuant to which the tenant agrees it will recognize the mortgagee as landlord.
Subrogation	• Subrogation refers to an insurance company seeking reimbursement from the person or entity legally responsible for an accident after the insurer has paid out money on behalf of its insured. It is the substitution of one creditor for another such that the substituted person succeeds to the legal rights and claims of the original claimant. Typically, leases have clauses waiving this right.

CLAUSE	DESCRIPTION
Tenant Improvements	• This clause details the amount of money the tenant is granted by the owner to spend on improvements to their space before they open.
	• The standard allowance for a given office is set by the owners separate and apart from any other concessions and is based on a dollar amount per square foot.
	• A work letter agreement may identify a certain number of building standard components that are allowed for a given square footage of leased space, such as electrical outlets, light fixtures, interior walls, or other fixed installations using building standard materials.
	• The lease should have attached to it an exhibit that outlines exactly what the tenant will receive as the bare shell space and how the costs for the improvements to the space will be divided between tenant and owner.
Utilities	• The tenant is required to pay utilities billed directly for the leased premises, and the landlord may bill the tenant for a pro rata share of utilities not metered directly to the tenant's space.
	• Electricity and gas are typically provided from private sources and billed directly, while water is usually a municipal service to the property with sewer charges based on water use.
	• Waste disposal (trash pickup, recycling) may be treated as a utility or addressed separately, depending on how the service is contracted. Some tenants have special disposal needs that may have to be addressed individually (e.g., health professionals' wastes would be considered a biohazard).

Q&A: Lease Clauses

Q. How do you address items that are negotiated in a building's standard lease?

A. This depends on management company best practices, intent of parties, and the brokerage firm. Consider showing all changes in an addendum to the lease rather than within the body of the lease. Since the real estate manager, not the broker, has to administer the lease, it is important to ensure that all items are appropriately addressed and easily identified.

Retail Lease Provisions

The following retail lease provisions should be added to the office lease as necessary.

CLAUSE	DESCRIPTION
Sales Reporting and Sales Audit	• Percentage rent is based on sales volume, so tenants are required to submit periodic (usually monthly) reports of sales, usually in a format specified by the landlord.
	• This clause is also a provision for tenants' sales to be audited. Usually such audits are done by an outside service in such a way that some portion of the tenancy of the building is audited in any one year (the cost of auditing all tenants every year would be prohibitive).
	• Tenants whose reported sales never quite reach the breakpoint or whose stores have low sales levels despite good traffic may warrant auditing more frequently. Most leases provide for the tenant to pay the auditing costs if the audit finds additional percentage rent is due or sales are understated.
The "Use" Provision	• Every retail lease should specifically state the goods or services that the tenant intends to sell. Uses must be legal, and may or may not duplicate the uses of other tenants, depending on the tenant mix and objectives.
Signage	• Signage criteria should be established, including the landlord's right of approval; compliance with local laws may be an added consideration.
Store Hours	• Landlords want all tenants to maintain reasonable hours to maximize their sales. It is common to state the basic hours to be maintained, subject to extension for specific holidays.
Utilities and Janitorial	• The retail tenant is required to pay utilities billed directly for the leased premises, and the landlord may bill the tenant for a pro rata share of utilities not metered directly to the tenant's space (i.e., those master-metered to the building).
	• Electricity and gas are typically provided from private sources and billed directly while water is usually a municipal service with sewer charges based on water use.
	• Waste disposal (trash pickup, recycling) may be treated as a utility or addressed separately, depending on how the service is contracted.
	• Some tenants have special disposal needs that may have to be addressed individually: restaurants and supermarkets generate food wastes; pet stores dispose of animal excrement as well as feedstuffs; health professionals' wastes would be considered a biohazard.

Other Components

Aside from the basic components and numerous clauses, other elements may appear in an office lease, including:

- Options
- Guaranties
- Corporate resolution

OPTIONS

Options are sometimes negotiated for renewal, expansion, or cancellation of the lease. All options favor the tenant over the landlord and should not be granted without obtaining something in return.

OPTION	DESCRIPTION
Option to Renew	• May allow the tenant to renew its lease on the same terms or on some other terms as specified in the original lease
Option to Expand	• Provides the tenant with long-range growth; plans the opportunity to expand into additional (possibly adjacent) space after the expiration of (or during) the original lease term
	• Differs from a right of first refusal, which gives tenant first choice to lease contiguous or other space in the building if and when it becomes available
Option to Cancel	• Grants the tenant the right to terminate the lease before the expiration date if the owner cannot make additional space available as promised

GUARANTY

If a prospective tenant does not have sufficient credit, a *guaranty* may be required. A guaranty calls for the *guarantor* to pay all of the tenant's obligations to the owner in case the tenant defaults.

- This includes attorneys' fees for any action taken by the owner against the tenant
- The guarantor is not relieved of liability to the owner regardless of any modifications in the terms of the lease or any other agreements between the owner and the tenant
- The guarantor is still legally responsible for the lease if the tenant declares bankruptcy
- The owner is not obliged to inform the guarantor of any changes in his or her relationship with the tenant, any changes in the lease, or any other arrangements that may affect the payment of rent

- In the case of a small tenant, it is typically a personal guaranty with a list of assets attached and a salvo that any change must be reported, and breach is in effect if noncompliance occurs
- The actual certificate may be inserted with the exhibits at the back of the lease

CORPORATE RESOLUTION

In the case of a corporate entity, a resolution must be an addendum to the lease indicating the party allowed to enter into the lease (authorized by the corporation's board of directors), as well as the period and terms of the lease. The resolution must support any additional consideration for the duration of the lease.

LEASE NEGOTIATION

Every provision in an office lease is negotiable. Therefore, the standard lease form is only a starting point. Usually, concessions are made by both the tenant and the owner to reach mutually acceptable lease terms for all parties. The owner rarely participates directly in negotiations, which are the domain of the leasing agent and the prospective tenant, who may be represented by an agent or broker as well. Most negotiation discussions between the landlord and tenant focus on the following three items:

- Rent
- Term
- Tenant improvements

Preparing for Negotiations

The first step in preparing for negotiations is to examine your position and determine the *BATNA*, or Best Alternative to Negotiated Agreement. BATNA is the course of action that will be taken if an agreement cannot be reached. The following checklist provides some questions to help you arrive at your BATNA.

CHECKLIST: PREPARING FOR NEGOTIATIONS

☐ Can you find another tenant to fill the space?
☐ What concessions are acceptable to the owner?
☐ What are your strengths and weaknesses?
☐ What is the worst possible outcome that you will accept?
☐ What are the motivations and needs of the potential tenant?
☐ Is the tenant solvent? How long have they been in business?
☐ What are the tenant's priorities?
☐ What is the tenant willing to sacrifice?
☐ What would the tenant do if an agreement were not reached?

DO Determine items for discussion, the relative importance, and the extent to which the owner is comfortable negotiating each point. Know the NPV.

DON'T Assume you know the tenant's needs—determine needs through research, your own knowledge, tenants in the same industry, or others who have dealt with same tenant.

DO Design lease terms that are advantageous for the owner and that meet the tenant's needs.

DON'T Disclose what you would do if no agreement were reached, but be willing to share information that will further conversation and ensure tenant understands your key requirements.

DO Use active listening and verbal and nonverbal tactics to build rapport and advance the conversation.

DON'T Underestimate the power of posturing. For example, know your audience, show up on time, be prepared, review company's financial statement, use inclusive conversation, tactfully say no, define "firm" vs. "negotiable" items, never react emotionally, recognize different personality types and styles (e.g., generational, gender, and so forth).

DO Look for patterns in the types of concessions made and recognize what messages are being sent (e.g., rapid or large concessions undermine credibility of initial offer).

DON'T Forget to consider the lease expiration of neighboring tenants to avoid dead space.

DO Be creative with floor plate configurations.

DON'T Box yourself in and miss opportunities for other deals.

DO Remember that tenants talk—they will compare terms!

Impact of Concessions

Lease negotiation requires agreement and compromise, often resulting in concessions by negotiators for the landlord. The costs and benefits of individual concessions need to be evaluated. Over the long term, these concessions have an impact on the office building's cash flow and property value. Possible concessions and how their costs are calculated are listed below.

TOP TEN CONCESSIONS

1. Base Rent Reduction
2. Free Rent
3. Free Pass-Through Charges
4. Cap on Pass-Through Charges
5. Cap on CPI-based Rent Escalation
6. Percentage Rent Adjustments
7. Tenant Improvement Allowance
8. Options
9. Lease Term
10. Other Restrictive or Financial Provisions

BASE RENT REDUCTION

To determine the cost of a reduction in the base rent, subtract the actual rental rate from the projected rental rate. A stated monthly base rate would be multiplied by 12 to determine the annual loss.

(Projected Rental Rate – Actual Rental Rate) × 12
= Annual Loss

Example:

A reduction of $0.25/sq ft/yr would reduce the annual rent on 1,000 square feet of rentable area by $250. Over a 10-year lease term, the loss would total $2,500.

No matter how slow market conditions are, resist lowering the base rent. Changes in the base rent will change the fundamental rent structure and have ongoing effects on owner income for years.

tips

FREE RENT

The cost to the owner in this case is the amount of rent not received for the agreed-upon period. (Typically, the period of free rent would be applied at the beginning of the lease term.) If, for example, a five-year lease agreement called for one month's free rent for each year of the lease, the total rent collected for the term would be reduced by one-twelfth.

FREE PASS-THROUGH CHARGES

Tenant charges may not have to be paid for the period during which free rent is granted as a concession. This cost is the amount of each charge (taxes, insurance, utilities, and so forth) waived each month, multiplied by the number of months the charges are not paid.

> **Example:**
>
> If pass-through charges average $1.80 per square foot per year, the loss on a 10,000 square foot space in conjunction with five months' free rent would total $7,500 ($1.80 ÷ 12 = $0.15/sq ft/month; 10,000 × $0.15 = $1,500/month × 5 months = $7,500).

CAP ON PASS-THROUGH CHARGES

The amount of a tenant's contribution for one or all pass-through charges may be limited by placing a *cap* (ceiling, lid) on the total. Lease language might read: "Tenant will pay its pro rata share of operating expenses not to exceed a stated dollar amount per square foot per year." (A cap might also be expressed as a percentage—e.g., "not to exceed 3% of the prior year.") The cap may not be in force until later in the lease term.

> **Example:**
>
> Using a 10,000 square foot space and an $8.10 cap, with a projected incremental increase of $0.20/sq ft/yr, the cost of this concession over a five-year lease would total $9,000 (see accompanying computation) and lower the tenant's operating expenses an average of $0.18/sq ft/year of the lease ($9,000 ÷ 10,000 sq ft = $0.90/sq ft ÷ 5 yrs).
>
> **Sample Calculation of Cap on Pass-Through Charges**
>
> | Yr | Operating Expenses $/Sq Ft/Yr | Cap | Tenant's Pro Rata Share (×10,000) | Tenant's Actual Oper. Expenses (×10,000) | Annual Cost of the Concession |
> |----|------|------|---------|---------|--------|
> | 1 | $7.80 | $8.10 | $78,000 | $78,000 | -0- |
> | 2 | $8.00 | $8.10 | $80,000 | $80,000 | -0- |
> | 3 | $8.20 | $8.10 | $82,000 | $81,000 | $1,000 |
> | 4 | $8.40 | $8.10 | $84,000 | $81,000 | $3,000 |
> | 5 | $8.60 | $8.10 | $86,000 | $81,000 | $5,000 |
>
> **TOTAL COST: $9,000**

CAP ON CPI-BASED RENT ESCALATION

In a situation where annual rent increases are based on the increase in the Consumer Price Index (CPI), a tenant may be able to negotiate a cap on the adjustment to its rent. Lease language might read: "Tenant's base rent will be adjusted each year based on the increase in the CPI (for a stated geographic area or the national average), but in any year the increase from the preceding year shall not be greater than an agreed percent." Historical data can be used to project the percentage increase over the term of the lease, and the cost of this concession can be estimated by a computation similar to that for the cap on pass-throughs.

PERCENTAGE RENT ADJUSTMENTS

A prospective retail tenant who is likely to generate a high volume of sales may try to lower the amount of percentage rent due. They are more likely to negotiate a lower percentage rate than an artificial breakpoint.

A percentage rate reduction may be negotiated if a landlord wants to secure a long-term lease or encourage a new business venture. The cost of these types of concessions is calculated by estimating the tenant's sales and annual growth and the difference in percentage rent income based on different rates and the natural breakpoint.

TENANT IMPROVEMENT ALLOWANCE

If the landlord agrees to allow a dollar amount per square foot to pay for build-out of the tenant's leased space, the cost of this concession is the rate multiplied by the usable area of the office space. Specifics are documented separately in a work letter. This is typical of newly developed space leased as a shell. In previously occupied space, the landlord may refurbish the premises, in which case the property manager would be asked to seek bids from contractors, and the cost of the concession would be the amount of the contractor's bill. Depending on market conditions, the tenant may be expected to reimburse the landlord for part or all of this allowance. A set amount of additional rent each month is another alternative.

OPTIONS

Options grant the tenant the right to purchase or lease something at a future date for a specified price and terms. Options always benefit the tenant rather than the owner. Options can affect both the owner's immediate cash flow and the long-term value of the property. Because long-term options tend to hold rents to a certain rate over a number of years, buyers and investors are less likely to pay a premium price for a property burdened with them.

The decision to build options into a lease often depends on the market conditions at the time. In a slow market, the owner may be more willing to grant a prospective tenant greater privileges regarding renewal and expansion options. Options should not be granted unconditionally or be extended to assignments/subletting.

In fairness to the owner, the lease statement granting options should require for their exercise that:

- The tenant must not be in default of the lease
- The tenant must give the owner written notice a specific period in advance
- Only the original tenant can exercise the option

LEASE TERM

The owner's preference will usually be for a longer lease term that includes provisions for the owner to raise rent in line with changing market conditions. The prospective tenant's preference will be for a shorter lease term with an option to renew at a fixed rate. A longer lease term can benefit both parties because it provides the tenant a measure of security and guarantees the owner a steady income with which to service debts and accumulate capital. On the other hand, options to renew at a fixed rate are granted only rarely and then usually only to major tenants.

LEASE ANALYSIS

Effective Rent

The *effective rent* is the total rent over the term of the lease. Calculating effective rent (especially on commercial leases) is rarely as simple as multiplying the rental term by the rental rate. Often, you have to consider the following:

- Periods of free or reduced rent
- Allowances for tenant improvements
- Brokerage commissions
- Buy out incentives such as prior lease buy out or early termination option
- Time value of money because you are setting today the amount of money you will receive in the future

Example:

Let's say a one-month period of free rent is granted to the tenant. The landlord is offering $15 per usable square foot to finish a 3,000 usable square foot shell space. The lease calls for base rent of $15 per rentable square foot per year for a period of three years. The building has an R/U factor of 1.12. As it turns out, the tenant finish costs are actually $25 per usable square foot. Broker commissions of 5% are paid by the landlord. Any negotiated concessions (free rent, additional tenant improvement allowance, and so forth) will impact the effective rent collected.

Without giving consideration to the time value of money, effective rent for both tenant and landlord is calculated below. Note that discounted cash flow techniques and consideration of the time value of money are explored in detail in the IREM "Investment Real Estate Financing and Valuation—Part Two (ASM604)" course.

Tenant's Effective Rent

Tenant improvements	3,000 usf × $25.00	$75,000
Less: landlord contribution	3,000 usf × $15.00	– 45,000
		30,000
Rent:	3,000 usf × 1.12 R/U factor = 3,360 rsf	
	3,360 rsf × $15.00 × 3 years	$151,200
Less: free rent	3,360 rsf × $15.00 ÷ 12	– 4,200
Total rent paid by tenant		$147,000
Effective rent:	$30,000 + $147,000	$177,000
Average annual effective rent/rsf		
	$177,000 ÷ 3 years ÷ 3,360 rsf	$17.56

Landlord's Effective Rent

Landlord TI contribution	3,000 usf × $15.00	$45,000
Rent:	3,000 usf × 1.12 R/U factor = 3,360 rsf	
	3,360 rsf × $15.00 × 3 years	$151,200
Less: free rent	3,360 rsf × $15.00 ÷ 12	– 4,200
Total rent received by landlord		$147,000
Less: brokerage commissions	$147,000 × 5%	7,350
Effective rent:	$147,000 - $45,000 - $7,350	$94,650
Average annual effective rent/rsf:		
	$94,650 ÷ 3 years ÷ 3,360 rsf	$9.39

Don't forget that *closing*, or the signing of the lease by all parties, is an expected part of the negotiation process. It is the natural culmination of your marketing and leasing efforts. Various approaches include:

- "If I could, would you?" (i.e., offering a concession and asking tenant to sign)
- Emphasize the pros over the cons
- Mention other tenants who have signed

Comparative Lease Proposals

Lease proposals, or *Letters of Intent,* can be submitted from tenant to landlord, and from landlord to tenant. When assessing comparative lease proposals as a landlord, it is important to consider issues such as:

- What the proposed tenant's use will do for the building
- How the tenant will fit with the tenant mix
- How credit worthy each tenant prospect is

On a comparative basis, a lease proposal may include rental rates (base and additional rents), amount of security deposit, lease term, options, tenant obligations, landlord obligations, taxes, and insurance. The proposal may also include site plans, photographs, and other exhibits. A deadline date for the prospect to accept the proposal should be clearly outlined.

Proposed tenants should be compared and ratings should be given to each of their features. Assign a weight to each feature based on its importance to the landlord. The weighted features should then be evaluated to determine the best tenant for the space.

Publications:

The Dollars & Cents of Shopping Centers. Urban Land Institute, 2008.

Websites:

www.bls.gov (U.S. Department of Labor's Bureau of Labor Statistics)

CHAPTER 5:
Resources

www.boma.org (Building Owners and Managers Association [BOMA])

CHAPTER 6

Retaining Tenants

This book follows the typical timeline of an office building lease deal. The timeline below shows where we are within the process.

Understanding Office Buildings	Assessing the Market	Developing Marketing Plans	Developing Leasing Plans	Formulating the Lease	**Retaining Tenants**

The real estate manager can reduce turnover, maintain occupancy, and meet the owner's goals by implementing a tenant retention program. A property manager must be able to explore tenant retention strategies and techniques for investigating and resolving complaints.

What's in this chapter:

- Lease Renewal Strategy
- Implementing Retention Strategies
- Resolving Problems
- Lease Expiration and Lease Buy Outs

LEASE RENEWAL STRATEGY

Real estate, like other industries, is cyclical in nature. Real estate cycles are a result of imbalances between supply and demand and a reaction to the general business economy. Economic cycles in business are typically triggered by a variety of influences, including variations in international money exchange, trade deficits, government debt, and monetary and fiscal policies.

The business cycle has four stages:

- **RECESSION:** Slowdown in business activity
- **DEPRESSION:** Widespread reduction in business activity, increased unemployment rates, lower wages, and a decline in stock values
- **RECOVERY:** Unemployment rate falls, wages may increase, consumer demand returns, and prices climb
- **PROSPERITY:** Businesses begin to see higher profits, production is increased, banks are willing to lend funds as a result of business expansion, and consumer demand is at a high, as are prices

In response to the business cycle, the real estate market rises and falls in four major phases that lag behind the business cycle. The peaks and valleys of the real estate cycle are typically more pronounced and can be characterized as the following stages:

- Overbuilding
- Adjustment
- Stabilization
- Development

Leasing practices vary based on business and real estate trends. For example, during cycles of prosperity, managers may see more lease buy outs and tenant expansions. However, during cycles of recession, managers may see more "blend and extend" transactions. Also, lease terms and option periods may be more conservative during challenging economic times because the owner (and/or tenant) does not want to get locked into unfavorable rates for longer than necessary (e.g., 5-year term vs. 10-year term, or a -year fixed term with an option for an additional two years as opposed to five years).

The real estate cycle has pronounced peaks and valleys because real estate is not a liquid or fluid investment. In comparison to alternative investments such as stocks or bonds which can immediately be bought or sold, the real estate transaction is lengthy and encumbers the investment for specified periods. For example, a development once begun cannot be easily stopped, and sale transactions are typically not completed in days but weeks or months.

FIGURE 6-1: BUSINESS AND REAL ESTATE CYCLES

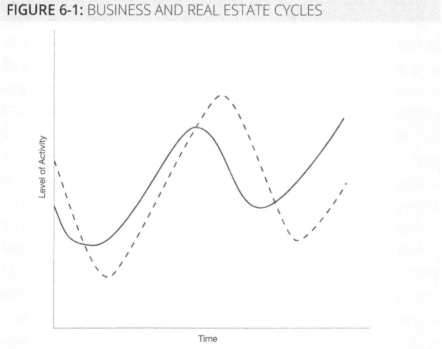

The solid line indicates the business cycle and the broken line shows the real estate cycle, which responds to the cycle of business and has more pronounced peaks and valleys.

IMPLEMENTING RETENTION STRATEGIES

Retaining existing tenants is important because it helps owners and managers avoid the expense and effort of tenant turnover. Loss of a tenant impacts:

- Pro forma projections of net operating income
- Rate of return on investment for the property owner

It is important to develop wide and deep relationships with building tenants. That way, when or if your primary contact leaves the firm, you still have other significant relationships on which to draw.

tips

Additionally, renewing an existing lease is more profitable than finding a new tenant for the following reasons:

- Avoids marketing and leasing costs
- Avoids leasing commission costs
- Costs less to improve space for current tenant than preparing vacated space for a new tenant
- Maintains established relationship with current tenant (must be established all over again with new tenant)
  - Favorable payment history
  - Respect for property and neighboring tenants
- Creates loyal customers and promotes positive word-of-mouth advertising and referrals

Every interaction with the tenant's personnel, from move-in through the expiration of the lease term, is an opportunity to encourage subsequent lease renewals and foster tenant retention. Keep in mind that tenant retention is a process, not an event.

tips

Communication

Constant communication with tenants and great customer service are the best ways to avoid complaints. Consider the following strategies:

- Prepare new tenant kit for move-in with welcome letter and visit
- Encourage management team to routinely walk the property and be approachable
- Provide necessary management contact information, encourage tenants to get in touch, and respond promptly

Example:

Space Rented:	9,200 rentable square feet
Lease Expires in	9 months
Lease Term:	36 months
Rental Rate:	$25.00/sq ft
R/U Factor:	1.15
Pass-Though expenses	Triple-Net Lease= $9.50/rsf
TI Allowance:	$12.00/sq ft (remodel), $3.00/sq ft (renewal)
	(based on usable sq ft)
Time to Re-Lease:	6 months
Leasing Commission:	$1.15/sq ft (new), $0.38/sq ft (renewal)

Using this data, the following comparison can be made:

	Cost to Keep	Cost to Replace
Lost Revenue @ 6 Months	----	115,000
Loss of NNN @ 6 Months	----	43,700
Finish Allowance	24,000	96,000
Leasing Commission	10,488	31,740
Total Cost	$34,488	$286,440
Incremental Cost of Losing This Tenant	$251,952 →	7 times the cost to replace tenant

($251,952 ÷ $34,488 = 7.30)

- Use e-mails, phone calls, and personal visits to connect:
  - Explain unclear lease terms and building operations
  - Identify potential problems or complaints
  - Observe the office operations and personnel
  - Consider tenant suggestions for building improvements
- Distribute building newsletter (announce scheduled construction, upcoming events, or other news)
- Hold periodic tenant meetings and publish summary

Facilitating Tenant Success

The office environment, technology and automation, and space planning tools are becoming increasingly important aspects of tenant retention. Customer appreciation events, curb appeal, customer service, and staff training continue to be important to tenant retention as well.

Jacqueline Harris, CPM
Los Angeles, California

Case Study: Casual Check-ins

One of the things I've found most helpful in communicating with tenants is the casual, yet frequent, check-in. Sometimes this means an impromptu cup of coffee, and other times it is simply part of "Friday Rounds." I've found that this technique is a great way to build relationships and show tenants that I'm "hands on," available, and care about the office park. It is amazing how much more you can learn about the pulse of a tenant's business, their industry, or changes in management when things are casual. I often learn valuable information from the assistant and other staff. Ultimately, this technique provides insights on the optimal time to talk about lease renewals and allows me to recognize when available space may suit a tenant's needs better. The more you know about your tenants, the more equipped you will be to successfully meet their needs and encourage lease renewals.

ENVIRONMENT

A good environment allows employees to function in a professional, efficient manner, which helps business performance. Therefore, tenants may demand more requirements regarding indoor air quality, lighting efficiency, and HVAC control.

TECHNOLOGY

Tenants want the latest, state-of-the-art communications systems, high-speed Internet access, and automated tools to communicate with management and succeed at their business. Web-based applications that automate tenant service requests boost customer service response levels, which helps management retain tenants as well as attract new ones.

SPACE PLANNING

Another important retention tool is space planning. An otherwise satisfied tenant may relocate to a different building because the current space can no longer accommodate expansion. This scenario is less likely to happen if the tenant and building manager maintain constant contact and the building manager keeps in tune with the tenant's future space needs. For the tenant, this contact helps ensure that facilities are available at the right time, in the right place, at the right cost. For the building manager and owner, this contact helps anticipate and accommodate space requirements of major tenants without lost revenues.

APPRECIATION EVENTS

There are many ways to show appreciation for your tenants and to create an atmosphere of camaraderie in the building. See the following checklist for some suggestions:

- ☐ Anniversary gift (card, floral arrangement)
- ☐ Lunch or dinner for tenant
- ☐ Themed luncheons (e.g., Mexican)
- ☐ Barbecue
- ☐ Ice cream day
- ☐ Holiday parties
- ☐ Health fair
- ☐ Casino event
- ☐ Giveaways (gift certificates and coupons)
- ☐ Golf tournament
- ☐ Sporting league
- ☐ Art display
- ☐ Recycling event (e.g., cell phones, light bulb exchange, earth day)
- ☐ Charitable events (e.g., holiday canned food drive, blood drive, breast cancer awareness)
- ☐ Recognition gift if tenant is honored by their industry or profiled in publications such as Forbes

CURB APPEAL

A property's appearance and overall condition have an obvious effect on tenant retention. Tenants want to feel proud of where they work—ego and sense of status are not to be ignored. Complaints about the appearance of the property, the quality and frequency of interior and exterior maintenance and repairs, or management services in general should be taken seriously. If you ignore these indications of dissatisfaction, you could lose your existing tenants.

CUSTOMER SERVICE

There are two levels of customer service:

- **MINIMUM EXPECTATION** that the leased area will be clean, presentable, and in good working condition.
- **SERVICE EXPECTATION** that management will ensure high-quality and timely repairs in the leased space so tenants may conduct their business operations. Timeliness is measured in terms of whether the work was done immediately or put off until later. Make sure to understand and respond appropriately to "special" circumstances (open house/grand opening event, corporate headquarters meeting, governmental/permit inspections, and so forth).

Tenants also factor in how they are treated each time they come into contact with building management—whether their concerns were received with courtesy or with rudeness or indifference. A *moment of truth* can be defined as any episode in which the customer comes into contact with any aspect of the organization and gets an impression of the quality of its service.

- A **PASSIVE MOMENT OF TRUTH** is one that is inherent in the business of real estate management
  - Examples: cleaning service, service requests, routine tasks, deferred maintenance
- An **ACTIVE MOMENT OF TRUTH** is one that is created intentionally
  - Examples: morning coffee/bagel giveaways, repaving the parking lot, building repairs

"Make comment cards available during building-wide events. Tenants are more likely to tell you about the bad stuff when they feel good. And, remember that tenants talk, so standard gifts are best to avoid any perception issues."

– Jacqueline Harris, CPM, Los Angeles, California

STAFF TRAINING

You may develop the best tenant retention program for your property, but it will not be successful unless you also have in place a properly selected and trained staff dedicated to providing the tenants with the best service. Provide ongoing training, encouragement, and recognition for individual employees' accomplishments. Empower your employees to solve problems without being constrained by rules and procedures.

Technical competence and people-friendly orientation are different skill sets. You can provide technical training, but you may not be able to train a technically competent candidate to be a "people person."

tips

RESOLVING PROBLEMS

Determining and promptly addressing areas of tenant dissatisfaction will reinforce your commitment to the tenant and highlight areas of the property or management practices that may need to be improved.

Responding to Complaints

Tenants will find various ways to communicate when they are not satisfied with the service management provides. Service requests will always be an operational issue, but it is important to remember complaints and issues should be addressed promptly and courteously. Welcoming tenant complaints can help:

- Retain tenants who might have chosen to move
- Alert management to areas that need improvement

- Minimize negative word-of-mouth feedback to other tenants
- Provide a learning experience in complaint-handling

Soliciting Feedback

To determine tenant satisfaction with the property, you must solicit their feedback. This can be done formally by asking the tenant to complete a questionnaire or informally by having a face-to-face conversation. Consider posting the questionnaire to a website and allowing occupants to anonymously complete the survey. Surveys should be conducted on regular intervals, and especially upon exit. It is important to understand why you lost a tenant and if any factors were in your control.

USING THE RESULTS

Soliciting feedback is fruitless unless you do something with the data you collect. Remember that by giving tenants an opportunity to provide feedback, you establish in their minds an expectation that steps will be taken to resolve any issues. Periodically assess your results:

- Identify trends from year to year
- Recognize gaps in performance
- Develop a plan to address issues and concerns
- Prioritize focus areas
- Budget for maintenance and repairs
- Assess opportunities for new business
- Understand when a change is necessary
- Identify performance management goals
- Establish new benchmarks—expect continual improvement and celebrate success
- Forecast occupancy in future years

FIGURE 6-2: EXAMPLE SURVEY RESULTS

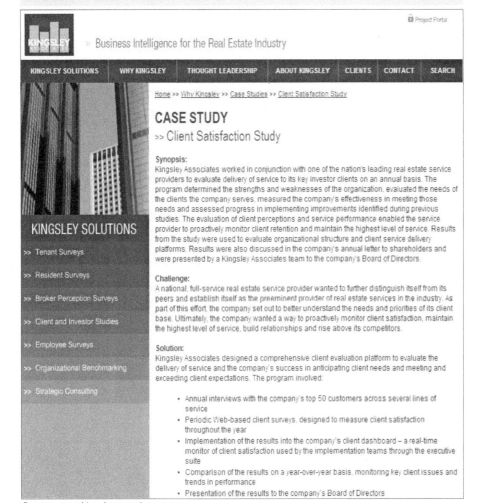

Source: www.kingsleyassociates.com

FIGURE 6- 3: SAMPLE TENANT SURVEY

Tenant Name   Suite Number _____

Survey Completed by   Date _____

We value your opinion, and we need your help to ensure that the management of [building name] continues to meet your expectations in providing requested services. We therefore ask you to take a few moments to answer the questions below and return this form to the management office. Thank you very much.

Please rate the following service categories on a scale of 1 to 5, where 1 = superior, 2 = above average, 3 = average, 4 = below average, and 5 = unsatisfactory. For items that are not applicable, circle NA.

Janitorial Service—In your office area	1	2	3	4	5	NA
Janitorial Service—Corridors and lobbies	1	2	3	4	5	NA
Janitorial Service—Rest rooms	1	2	3	4	5	NA
Overall maintenance of landscaped areas	1	2	3	4	5	NA
HVAC operations	1	2	3	4	5	NA
Elevator operations	1	2	3	4	5	NA
Security procedures	1	2	3	4	5	NA
Parking—For employees	1	2	3	4	5	NA
Parking—For visitors	1	2	3	4	5	NA
Building amenities	1	2	3	4	5	NA
Tenant communication	1	2	3	4	5	NA

Please rate the members of the management team listed below, using the same scale.

Building Manager

Responsiveness	1	2	3	4	5	NA
Courtesy	1	2	3	4	5	NA
Follow-through	1	2	3	4	5	NA

Maintenance Team

Responsiveness	1	2	3	4	5	NA
Courtesy	1	2	3	4	5	NA
Follow-through	1	2	3	4	5	NA

Security Personnel

Responsiveness	1	2	3	4	5	NA
Courtesy	1	2	3	4	5	NA
Follow-through	1	2	3	4	5	NA

Please comment specifically on the following areas:

What would you suggest to improve energy management in the building?

What would you suggest to improve building operations in general?

Will you need expansion space within the next 6 months? 12 months? 18 months? 24 months? ____

Other Comments _____
_____
_____

Lease Violations

A tenant may be in violation of the lease for many reasons. For example:

- Non-payment of rent
- Violating the intended use
- Disrupting other tenants' work, perhaps due to equipment noise or other behavior
- Subletting a portion of the space or the entire space without management knowledge or approval
- Bringing pets to work
- Disregarding housekeeping and maintenance guidelines

In order to prevent lease violations, it is important to maintain good relationships and open communication. You must stress why you want to monitor the lease carefully as well as the rationale for each lease term. Ultimately, the goal is to protect yourself and the owner's investment. It is also helpful to explain the consequences of default such as the loss of free/reduced rent and options.

The procedures for lease violations are regulated by state statute. For example, in California it is legal to accept late rent checks when planning to evict a tenant, but that practice is prohibited in other areas. Check with your legal counsel before taking any action to evict.

Legal Issue

In the case of a lease violation, consider the following:

- Handle the issue tactfully.
- Explain the reasons for the lease provision so that the tenant understands the importance of abiding by the terms of the lease.
- Be persistent and maintain a log of your contact attempts if you cannot get in touch with the tenant if rent is late.
  - If the tenant claims the check has been mailed, ask for the account number and offer to contact the bank to trace the status of the check.

- If a collection letter must be used, it should be polite and appeal to the tenant's sense of fairness, urgency, and fear of legal issues. Do not send a letter of default unless you intend to follow through on it.
- Do not accept a late rent check if you plan to evict a tenant for late rent payments. Notify your legal department or attorney immediately if a delinquent check has been received—holding onto the check, even if you do not deposit it, may be interpreted by the tenant as acceptance of the check.
- Document, document, document. Letters to the tenant or to the file create information needed to take additional action and if necessary, to initiate legal proceedings to protect the owner's interest.

FIGURE 6-4: CONSIDERATIONS BEFORE FINDING THE TENANT IN DEFAULT

☐ Is the building better off if the space is occupied for the time being, even if the tenant pays no rent?
☐ How damaging would a vacancy be?
☐ What are the costs of tenant turnover?
☐ Is trying to save an existing tenant more efficient than searching for a new one?

LEASE EXPIRATION AND BUY OUTS

The success of an office building depends largely on its ability to respond to changes in tenants' needs and to remain competitive with neighboring buildings. Building managers should always be aware of the financial condition of their tenants and the trends of their tenants' industries. This allows managers to be on the look-out for opportunities to replace weak tenants before they vacate. Leasing should be regarded as an ongoing activity—renewal and replacement leasing before lease expiration will help ensure your tenant mix remains profitable for the building.

Lease Renewal

Lease renewal is a process, not an event. Lease renewal begins the day the tenant moves into your property. The act of initiating a renewal lease agreement should take place long before a tenant's lease expiration date. One of the first things an agent should be aware of is how much of the rentable space in the building is represented by leases that will expire within a certain period of time. Keep in mind the following considerations during the lease renewal process:

- Which leases have a fixed-rate option or no option at all?
  - A tenant without a fixed-rate option must renegotiate the lease, usually with a rent increase based on an escalation index (CPI) or on market rates
  - An owner interested in increasing the rental income of a property will be more concerned with tenants that do not have a fixed-rate renewal option

- Do lease expirations represent contiguous spaces? How many square feet will be vacant at the same time?
- Do any upcoming lease expirations have any expansion rights attached to them?

Because office leases are typically for a term longer than one year and may involve complicated negotiations, renewal notification may be given six months to a year or more before lease expiration. Changes in the lease terms, particularly increases in base rent and pass-through charges need to be explained and justified. The exact amount of a rental increase may be subject to negotiation depending on market conditions. In such instances, the negotiations may be as comprehensive as for a new lease.

Expansion

Adding space to a building is another way to make a building more profitable as well as increase its value. If the *expansion* is to create a larger space for a single tenant, it may be appropriate to charge different rental rates for the new space as compared to the old one. The cost of the new construction must be factored into the negotiations.

If the landlord is asking the tenant to pay for tenant improvements, to compensate for the new tenant's upfront investment, the base rent for the new space may be set lower than the rate set for the existing space, although that rate should account for improvements to the old space if they were made. Having varied rental rates can allow the new tenant to operate profitably while sharing part of the cost of the construction. The building owner will benefit immediately, from the increased rental income on the larger total leasable space, and long term, from the substantial increase to the value of the building.

Blend and Extend

When economic conditions are bad, a viable option for negotiating lease renewals can be to *blend and extend.* Basically, this approach takes the tenant's current lease rate, lowers it to a market rate, and extends the lease terms. Essentially, this combines the old rate and old term with the new rate and new term. A blend and extend may be the only way to keep a tenant that is in distress, but it will impact the building's value. The real estate manager must examine the financial impact of this approach and ensure it is in line with the owner's goals and a true "win-win" situation. Note that blend and extends can be done without broker involvement, which reduces or eliminates commission cost on the extended term.

Buy out

When a tenant's presence no longer contributes to the overall success of an established building and another tenant is eager to rent that space, the most beneficial negotiation alternative may be for a landlord to offer to buy out a tenant's lease. A *buy out* involves paying the tenant a sum of money to break its lease. When the rent an owner could receive for a given space is considerably greater than the rent a current tenant is paying, a buy out can be very effective. At times a tenant will vacate with the knowledge that their lease will be terminated and they will not be obligated to pay rent through their original term. A discussion of replacing a tenant should always be the first step before any monetary incentive is offered. If this is not successful, a buy out may be necessary. Essentially, a buy out is a technique to induce and compensate a tenant to leave.

LANDLORD-INITIATED BUY OUT

Example:

Blackstone Publishing occupies 2,500 square feet of office space. Blackstone has a five-year lease with one year remaining. Under the lease, base rent is $9.00/sq ft/yr, there is no escalation provision. Pro rata pass-through expenses (taxes, insurance, maintenance) total $3.80/sq ft/yr. Rent and charges total $32,000 per year ($12.80 × 2,500 sq ft). Blackstone is willing to terminate if the owner will pay $7,500 to buy out its lease.

A prospective tenant, Velvet Touch Interior Designs, has been identified and signed to a lease contingent on Blackstone vacating the premises. Velvet Touch is willing to pay $14.00/sq ft/yr in base rent (pass-throughs are unchanged). It would take Velvet Touch one month to construct its own tenant improvements (with no allowance from the landlord) and move in. During that one month, Velvet Touch would pay no rent or pass-throughs.

To determine whether the owner will benefit by buying out Blackstone's lease and re-leasing the space to Velvet Touch Interior Designs, you will need to calculate the difference in total base rent and the amount of lost income. (The lost income is only for a period of one month.)

Velvet Touch's proposed rent ($/sq ft/yr)	$ 14.00
minus Blackstone's actual rent ($/sq ft/yr)	- 9.00
Increase in rent ($/sq ft/yr)	**$ 5.00**
times Office space (sq ft)	× 2,500
Total increase in rent	**$12,500.00**
Lost base rent ($/sq ft/month)	$ 0.75 ($9.00 ÷ 12)
plus Lost pass-throughs ($/sq ft/month)	+ 0.32 ($3.80 ÷ 12)
Total lost income ($/sq ft/month)	**$ 1.07**
times Office space (sq ft)	× 2,500
Total income lost (for one month)	**$ 2,675.00**
Total increase in rent	$12,500.00
minus Total lost income	- 2,675.00
minus Buy out payment	- 7,500.00
Net difference (first year)	**$ 2,325.00**

The owner would benefit by $2,325 in the first year.

TENANT-INITIATED BUY OUT

Sometimes a tenant may approach a landlord and offer to buy out of its lease. Tenants may find the location unprofitable and seek buy out. In other cases, the business could simply be relocating. The following is an example of a tenant-initiated lease buy out.

Example:

Ada's Advertising is a small company with about 30 employees. It occupies 7,000 square feet of office space on a seven-year lease with two years remaining. The lease calls for base rent of $8.25/sq ft/yr, with no escalation provision. The company is doing well, so the owner, Ms. Ada Abramov, would like to expand to 10,000 square feet, but the office park can't accommodate the expansion. Ada found desirable space in a new location, and the new landlord is willing to pay Ada an amount equal to a lump-sum discount based on the remaining rent so she can pay the current landlord and terminate the lease. What factors should be considered?

When considering lease expiration and renewal approaches, the real estate manager must understand the lease's impact on the value of the asset. Not every lease is a good lease.

tips

Websites:

www.irem.org/resources/by-topic/leasing (IREM Resources: Leasing)

CHAPTER 6:
Resources

APPENDIX A: LIST OF CALCULATIONS

CHAPTER 1: UNDERSTANDING OFFICE BUILDINGS

Pro Forma Statement:

   Gross Potential Income (GPI)
– Loss to Lease
– Vacancy and Collection Loss

= Net Rent Revenue
+ Miscellaneous Income
+ Expense Reimbursements

= Effective Gross Income (EGI)
– Operating Expenses

= Net Operating Income (NOI)
– Annual Debt Service (ADS)
– BLANK (Capital Expenditures or Reserves for Replacement)

= Before-Tax Cash Flow (BTCF)

Income Capitalization Approach (IRV):

Net Operating Income (I) ÷ Capitalization Rate (R)
= Estimated Market Value (V)

R/U Ratio:

Floor Rentable Area ÷ Floor Usable Area = Floor R/U Ratio

Basic Rentable Area = Usable Area × Floor R/U Ratio

Building R/U Ratio = Building Rentable Area ÷
(Building Rentable Area – Basic Rentable Area of Building Common Area)

R/U Ratio = Floor R/U Ratio × Building R/U Ratio

Rentable Area = Basic Rentable Area × Building R/U Ratio

CHAPTER 2: ASSESSING THE MARKET

Occupancy Rate

Amount of Occupied Space ÷ Total Amount of Available Space × 100 = Occupancy Rate

Vacancy Rate

Amount of Vacant Space ÷ Total Amount of Available Space × 100 = Vacancy Rate

Absorption

Square feet vacant at the beginning of the period
+ Square feet constructed new during the period
− Space demolished, or removed from the market by a change of use, during the period
− Space vacant at the end of the period
_____
= Space absorbed during the period (absorption)

Absorption Rate

Space Absorbed ÷ Total Supply of Available Space at the End of the Period = Absorption Rate

Market Share

Subject Square Feet ÷ Total Square Feet = X%

Break-Even Analysis

(Operating Expenses + Annual Debt Service) ÷ Gross Potential Income = Minimum Break-Even Point

Investor's Break-Even Analysis

(Operating Expenses + Annual Debt Service + *Return on Investment*) ÷ Gross Potential Income = Investor's Break-Even Point

CHAPTER 3: DEVELOPING MARKETING PLANS

Flat Percent Commission

Leased Sq Ft × Rent Rate × Length of Lease = Gross Rent
Gross Rent × % Rate = Commission

Dollars per Square Foot Commission

Leased Sq Ft × Rate = Commission

CHAPTER 4: DEVELOPING LEASING PLANS

Working Capital

Working Capital = Current Assets – Current Liabilities

Current Ratio

Current Ratio = Current Assets ÷ Current Liabilities

Net Worth

Net Worth = Total Assets – Total Liabilities

CHAPTER 5: FORMULATING THE LEASE

CPI Escalation

(CPI Current Year ÷ CPI Previous Year) × Current Monthly Rent = New Monthly Rent

Base Rent Reduction

(Projected Rental Rate – Actual Rental Rate) × 12 = Annual Loss

Effective Rent

Total rent over the term of the lease, considering:

- Periods of free or reduced rent
- Allowances for tenant improvements
- Brokerage commissions
- Buy out incentives such as prior lease buy out or early termination option
- Time value of money because you are setting today the amount of money you will receive in the future

Absorption: Net change in the amount of occupied space from one period to the next, normally a year. (Chapter 2)

Absorption Rate: Determined by dividing the absorption of space by the total supply of available space in the market. (Chapter 2)

Active Moment of Truth: One that is created intentionally (e.g., morning coffee/bagels, giveaways, building repairs). (Chapter 6)

Add-on or Load Factor: Used to charge the tenant for a percentage of the common areas, so the total square footage leased is equal to the floor's rentable area. (Chapter 1)

Adwords (Google): Places a link and a short description of the link target on a Google search results page. Also known as "sponsored links," which are separate from the search results, these links can advertise your property with one or two sentences and a link to the property website. Includes "pay-per-click" and display advertising. (Chapter 3)

Annual Debt Service (ADS): Annual amount paid to service the debt on the property. (Chapter 1)

Availability Rate: Includes vacancies as well as space that is occupied but available (e.g., sublease space, buildings under construction). (Chapter 2)

Base Rent: Rent per rentable or usable square foot per year, usually paid in regular monthly installments. (Chapter 5)

Base Year Approach: The owner establishes the initial rent using existing levels of taxes, insurance, and maintenance. These costs are then built into the lease rental rate, and during the term of the lease, the owner pays the expenses up to the amount established in the base year. (Chapter 5)

BATNA, or Best Alternative to Negotiated Agreement: Course of action that will be taken if an agreement cannot be reached. (Chapter 5)

Blend and Extend: Takes the tenant's current lease rate, lowers it to a market rate, and extends the lease terms. (Chapter 6)

Brand: Overall concept created to reflect a "feel" or "perception" that your property creates. (Chapter 3)

Break-even Point: Occupancy rate at which rents are just sufficient to cover expenses and debt service. (Chapter 2)

Buy Out: Paying the tenant a sum of money to break its lease. A tenant-initiated buy out is when the tenant pays the owner a sum of money to break the lease. (Chapter 6)

Canvassing: Throws a wide net over a geographic area, and can be done face-to-face or over the phone. (Chapter 3)

Cash-on-Cash Rate of Return ($/$%): Measures investor's rate of return on the investment. (Chapter 1)

Class A: Most attractive and prestigious buildings that command the highest rents. (Chapter 1)

Class B: May be similar structurally to Class A, but cannot command highest rents due to less desirable location, amenities, and so forth. (Chapter 1)

Class C: Often located on the perimeter of the central business district (CBD) and provides basic facilities and services, thereby commanding less rent. (Chapter 1)

Classified Ads: Includes classified ads for local print newspapers, magazines, and trade journals, as well as their associated websites. Consists of smaller ads that are relatively inexpensive and have a standardized type and layout. (Chapter 3)

Cold Calling: Identifying a specific target audience (e.g., lawyers) and calling them. (Chapter 3)

Collateral Materials: Includes brochures, flyers, and portfolios that are passed out to prospective tenants, available for download on websites, or included in a direct marketing campaign. (Chapter 3)

Comparable Sales Approach Valuation Method: Uses recent sales of similar properties to determine value. (Chapter 1)

Comparison Grid Analysis: Compilation of data that allows comparison of the rents and features of similar office buildings. It is used to calculate market rents for your building and helps assure that a competitive schedule of rental rates is developed. (Chapter 2)

Computer-assisted Design and Drafting (CAD) Systems: Detailed space specifications. (Chapter 1)

Consumer Price Index (CPI): Index in which the cost of goods is compared across the country and used when considering lease escalations. (Chapter 5)

Corporation: Entity that is liable for obligations under a contract, although some personal liability may accrue to its officers or board of directors under certain circumstances. (Chapter 5)

Cost Approach Valuation Method: Bases property value on the cost to replace the improvements on the land plus the market value of the land itself. (Chapter 1)

Current Ratio: Shows the ability to pay current bills with funds on hand and indicates the company's liquidity. (Chapter 4)

Declining Percent Commission (also known as sliding scale commissions): Involves the broker being paid at a declining rate over the course of the lease term. (Chapter 3)

Demand: Measured by the amount of occupied space plus the amount of vacancy that is expected when market rents are stable. (Chapter 2)

Demography: Study of the various socioeconomic factors related to populations. (Chapter 2)

Depression: Widespread reduction in business activity, increased unemployment rates, lower wages, and a decline in stock values. (Chapter 6)

Discounted Cash Flow Valuation Method: Determines the present value of a property by discounting all the future fiscal benefits of the real estate over a predetermined holding period. Instead of using a capitalization rate, a discount rate is used. (Chapter 1)

Display Advertising: Ranges from large or small ads for your property placed on another Web or mobile page—ad sizes and position on page will vary. (Chapter 3)

Dollars Per Square Foot Commission: An agreed-upon rate is multiplied by the total square footage of the space. (Chapter 3)

Effective Rent: Total rent over the term of the lease. (Chapter 5)

Exclusive Broker Listing: Broker assured in writing that the owner will not deal with any other leasing agent without paying a fee to the original broker. (Chapter 3)

Expense Stop Approach: The costs for operating the building at a certain occupancy percentage are calculated and broken down to a square footage basis. This figure is then built into the rents; the owner is responsible for the established amount, and tenants pay any increases above that level for each year of the lease. (Chapter 5)

Flat Percent Commission: Broker is paid a fee based on the rent over the term of the lease multiplied by a negotiated percentage rate. (Chapter 3)

Flex Space Buildings: Single-story, may have limited mezzanine office space, and often located in business parks. (Chapter 1)

Floor Common Area: The areas on a floor such as washrooms, maintenance closets, mechanical rooms, and elevator lobbies that are used by more than one tenant on that floor. (Chapter 1)

Floor Usable Area: The sum of usable areas, store areas, and building common areas on a floor. (Chapter 1)

Garden Office Buildings: Usually a low-rise structure with one or two stories and no elevators. (Chapter 1)

General Partnership: Debts and liabilities shared by all of the general partners. (Chapter 5)

Government Buildings: With privatization of government established, there are more opportunities available to manage public buildings or lease space to government tenants. (Chapter 1)

Gross Lease: Tenant pays a fixed rent and the landlord is responsible for paying all property expenses (taxes, insurance, utilities, repairs). (Chapter 1)

Gross Potential Income (GPI): Income potential for the property, if it were fully leased at current market rentals. (Chapter 1)

Guaranty: Calls for the guarantor to pay all of the tenant's obligations to the owner in case the tenant defaults. (Chapter 5)

Income Capitalization Approach Valuation Method: Converts a future income stream (net operating income or NOI) to an estimate of value through a process known as capitalization. It is the market valuation of a property based upon a one-year, or multiple-year, projection of income. (Chapter 1)

Internal Marketing Report: Records the frequency of advertising (print ads, direct mailings, billboards, broadcast ads, Internet ads) public relations events, and canvassing. (Chapter 3)

Internal Rate of Return (IRR): Rate of return that equates the present value of the expected future cash flows to the initial capital invested. (Chapter 1)

Investor's Break-even Point: Covers an additional specified return on the investment. (Chapter 2)

Leasing Plan: Component of the broader, overall marketing plan and is intended to identify specific spaces within the building that are to be leased. (Chapter 3)

Limited Liability Corporation (LLC): Business structure with corporation and partnership qualities. (Chapter 5)

Limited Partnership: Each limited partner is usually financially liable only up to the value of his or her proportionate investment. (Chapter 5)

Loss to Lease: Difference between current rents and market rents for those rents that, for any reason, exist at below-market rates. (Chapter 1)

Market Analysis: An evaluation of the competition and the property's position in the marketplace. (Chapter 2)

Market Share: The subject property represents a percentage of the total supply in the market area; that percentage is used to determine the building's market share. Using that percentage measured against annual absorption for the submarket, you can predict the building's natural capture rate, or how long it will take to lease your vacant space. (Chapter 2)

Marketing Activity Report: Keeps the client informed of leasing activity such as active prospects, submitted proposals, and signed leases. (Chapter 3)

Marketing Plan: Used to advertise and relay information about the property for the purposes of attracting prospective tenants to the property (macroeconomic plan that provides marketing vision and goals). (Chapter 3)

Medical Office Buildings (MOB): Buildings whose space is leased primarily to medical and dental professionals. (Chapter 1)

Minimum Expectation: Level of customer service that assumes that the leased area will be clean, presentable, and in good working condition. (Chapter 6)

Miscellaneous Income and Expense Reimbursements: Can be from any source other than rents (e.g., parking). (Chapter 1)

Mixed-use (MXD) Buildings: Combines at least three different uses. (Chapter 1)

Moment of Truth: Any episode in which the customer comes into contact with any aspect of the organization and gets an impression of the quality of its service. (Chapter 6)

Multi-story: Buildings with multiple floors including low-rise and high-rise buildings. Guidelines are dependent on regional characteristics, city size, or local conception. (Chapter 1)

Multi-use Buildings: Combines two uses (e.g., office and retail). (Chapter 1)

Natural Breakpoint: Amount of gross sales at which the percentage rent equals the minimum rent. (Chapter 5)

Neighborhood Analysis (also known as a "micro market analysis"): More narrowly focused than a regional analysis. It should evaluate the economic conditions of the smaller area, including local employment, rent levels, and office vacancy rates. (Chapter 2)

Net Lease: Tenant pays a prorated share of some or all operating expenses (pass-through charges) and taxes in addition to base or minimum rent. (Chapter 1)

Net-net (NN or double-net): Tenant pays taxes, insurance, and possibly utilities and special assessments. (Chapter 1)

Net-net-net (NNN or triple -net): Tenant pays a prorated share of all operating expenses, taxes, insurance, utilities, and maintenance. (Chapter 1)

Net Operating Income (NOI): Represents the amount of money that remains after operating expenses are subtracted from effective gross income. (Chapter 1)

Net Present Value (NPV): Difference between the cost of an investment and the discounted present value of all anticipated future fiscal benefits of that investment. (Chapter 1)

Networking: Making use of business and professional contacts. (Chapter 3)

Net Worth: Total assets less total liabilities. (Chapter 4)

Nonexclusive (open) Broker Listing: Gives the owner the right to deal with other agents. (Chapter 3)

North American Industry Classification System (NAICS): Standard used by federal statistical agencies in classifying business establishments for the purpose of collecting, analyzing, and publishing statistical data related to the U.S. business economy. (Chapter 2)

Occupancy Rate: Amount of space that is occupied, expressed as a percentage of the total supply of office space. (Chapter 2)

Operating Expenses: Line-by-line expenses associated with the property. (Chapter 1)

Partnerships: More than one partner responsible for paying rents and meeting other financial obligations. (Chapter 5)

Passive Moment of Truth: One that is inherent in the business of real estate management (e.g., cleaning service, service requests). (Chapter 6)

Percentage Rent: For retailers, percentage rent involves the tenant paying the owner a percentage of gross sales in addition to the base rent, or the greater of the two. (Chapter 5)

Pipeline Report: New or large competing space coming on the market. (Chapter 3)

Press Releases: Short announcements that include relevant information such as who, what, when, where, and why. (Chapter 3)

Print Display: Offers a range of opportunity in display ad size and color; larger image and graphic space afford the opportunity to convey property brand, theme, or competitive advantage message; more expensive often used for newly developed or renovated properties during initial lease-up or with many available spaces

Prospect Report: Logs each prospect contacted about leasing space and additional points of contact with that prospect (phone calls, e-mails, visits, letters of intent, and leases out for signatures). (Chapter 3)

Prosperity: Businesses begin to see higher profits, production is increased, banks are willing to lend funds as a result of business expansion, and consumer demand is at a high, as are prices. (Chapter 6)

Provisions of the Office Lease: A comprehensive list of office building lease clauses is available in Chapter 5.

Public Relations (PR): Refers to any form of promotion that is not paid for, such as press releases and word-of-mouth endorsement. It is intended to increase awareness and build the image of the property. (Chapter 3)

Recession: Slowdown in business activity. (Chapter 6)

Recovery: Unemployment rate falls, wages may increase, consumer demand returns, and prices climb. (Chapter 6)

Region (also called the "macro market"): Market area in which changes in economic conditions are likely to affect the fiscal performance of a particular office building. Often, the region is defined as the metropolitan statistical area (MSA) in which a property is located. (Chapter 2)

Regional Analysis (also known as the "macro market analysis"): Determines the economic strength of the area in general, including employment information, per capita income, and types of businesses. (Chapter 2)

Rent Schedule: Outlines the current or desired rents for each space; it may include additional lease terms (extension options, rights of refusal, etc.). (Chapter 4)

Rentable Area of a Building: The entire interior floor area less vertical penetrations through the floor (elevators, stairways, ventilation shafts). (Chapter 1)

Rentable Area of a Tenant's Leased Office Space: The space on which the tenant pays rent (usually includes certain common areas). (Chapter 1)

Rollover Schedule: Shows lease expiration dates. (Chapter 4)

Search Engine Optimization (SEO): Considers how prospects search for space and seeks to improve the ranking of the property website in the search engine results page the prospect sees. (Chapter 3)

Service Expectation: Level of customer service that assumes management will ensure high-quality and timely repairs in the leased space so tenants may conduct their business operations. (Chapter 6)

Sole Proprietorships: One individual personally responsible for paying rents and meeting other financial obligations. (Chapter 5)

Space Planning: Consulting with the tenant to determine needed space. (Chapter 4)

Stacking Plan: Displays placement and square footage dimensions of all spaces, and the building as a whole. (Chapter 4)

Supply: Quantity of occupied and unoccupied space available in a particular real estate market at a given time. (Chapter 2)

Telemarketing: Direct telephone promotion that relies on lists available for sale from list brokers. (Chapter 3)

Theme: Images, ideas, or symbols that are used to convey either a time-based message that can be adjusted (e.g., seasonal themes) or a specific promotion of part of the property. (Chapter 3)

Usable Area of a Building: The rentable area less certain common areas shared by all tenants (washrooms, hallways, storage areas). (Chapter 1)

Usable Area of a Tenant's Leased Office Space: The area bounded by the partitions that separate one tenant's space from another (this may comprise portions of a floor, an entire floor, or multiple floors of a building). (Chapter 1)

Vacancy and Debt Collection Loss: Includes economic vacancy (e.g., concessions), physical vacancy, and delinquent rents. (Chapter 1)

Vacancy Rate: Amount of vacant space expressed as a percentage of the total supply of office space. (Chapter 2)

Value Enhancement: Expected value at the end of the holding period less the initial value of the investment and the cost of implementing the improvements. (Chapter 1)

Working Capital: Difference between total current assets and total current liabilities (anything that will convert to cash within the next 12 months). (Chapter 4)